FACES

Stev Peter

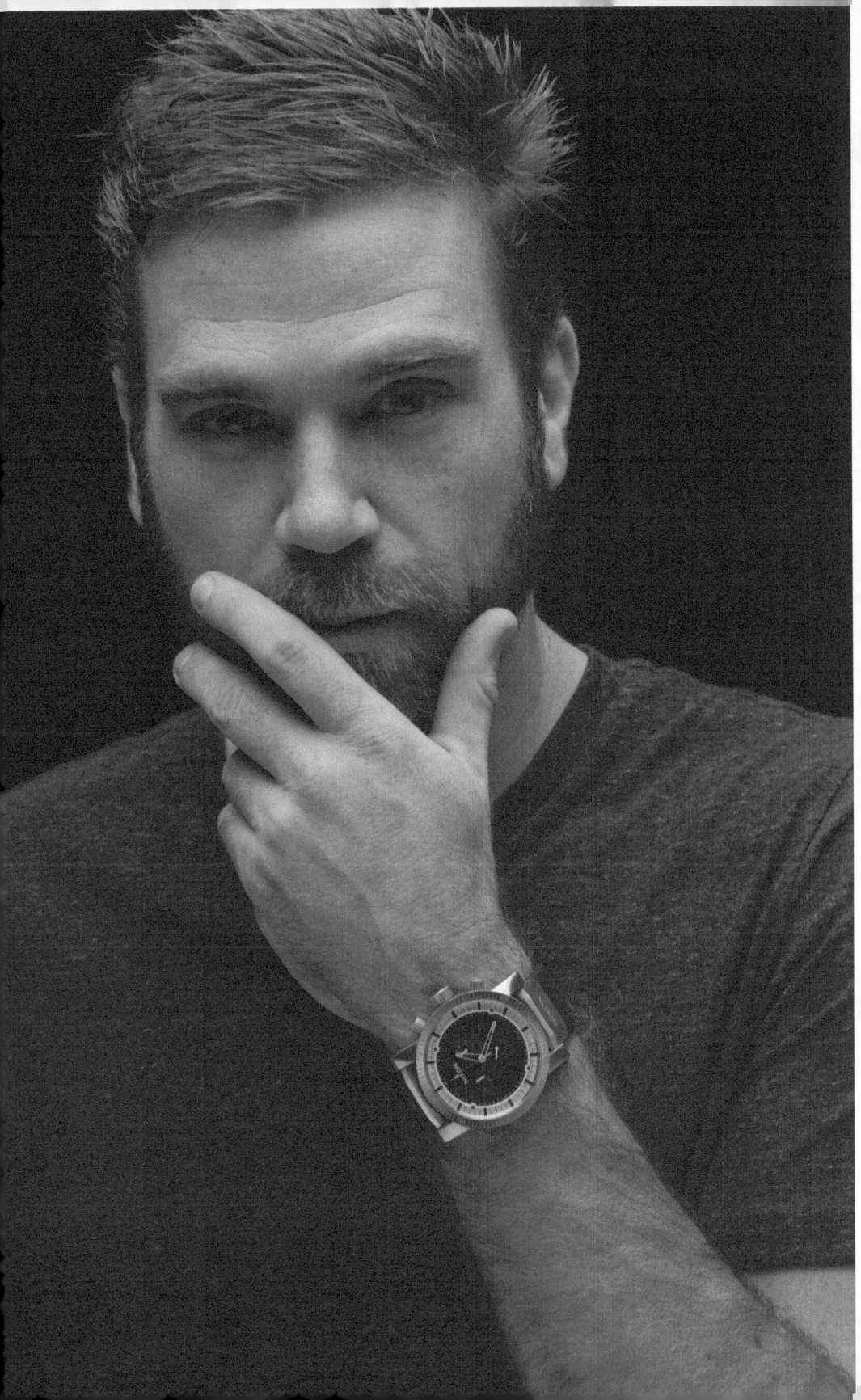

"Faces, all around different faces I see..."

Z Unlimited

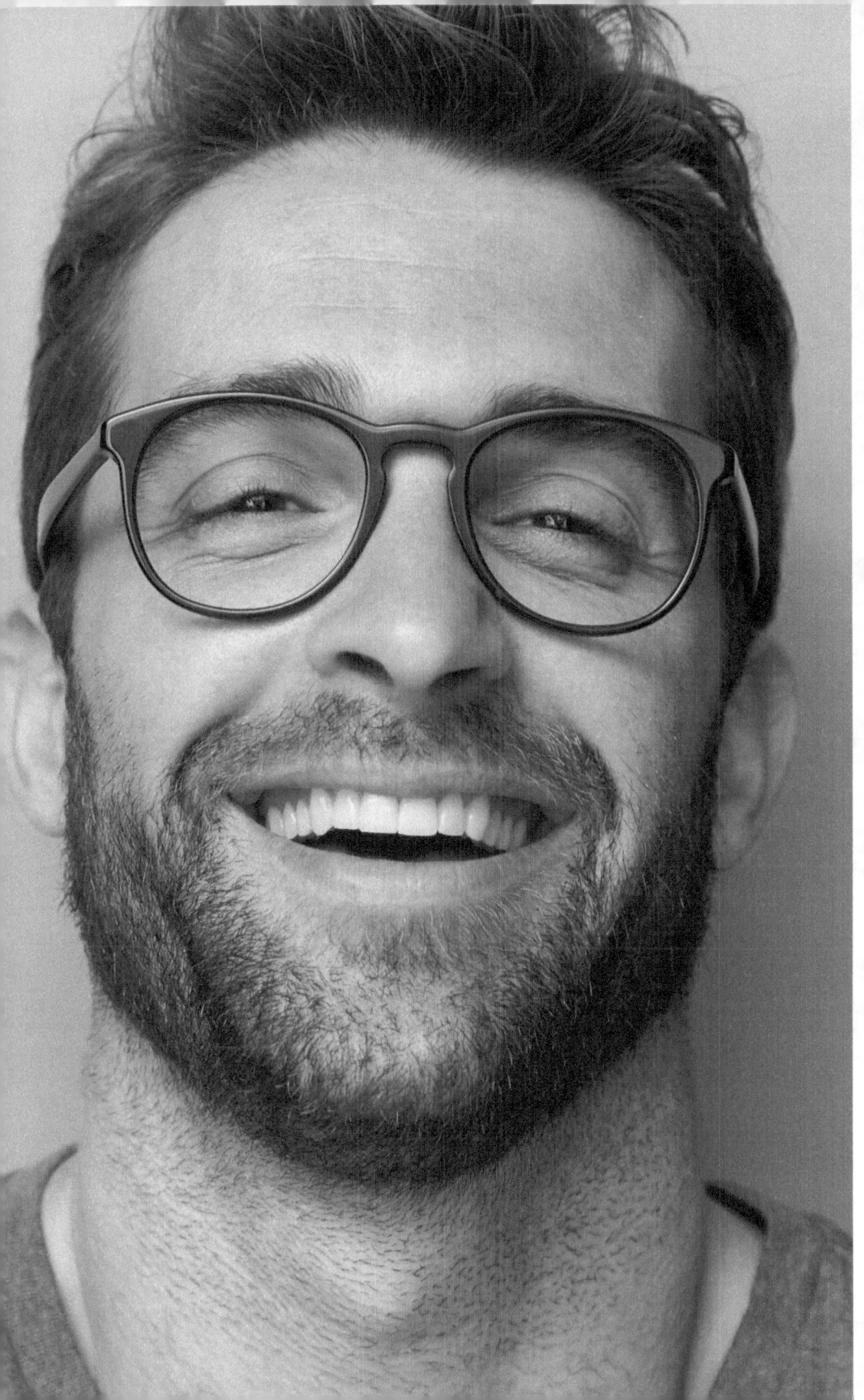

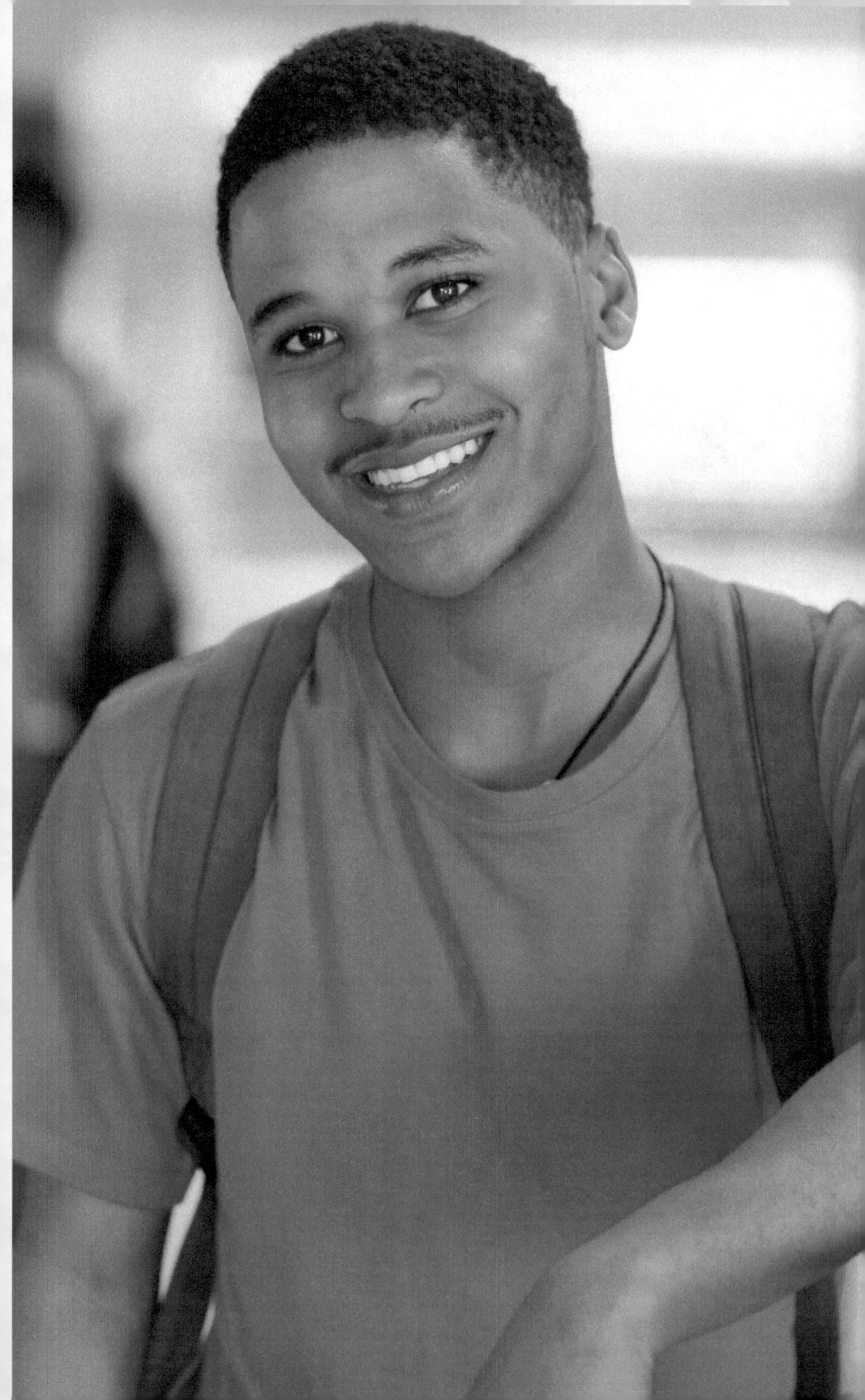

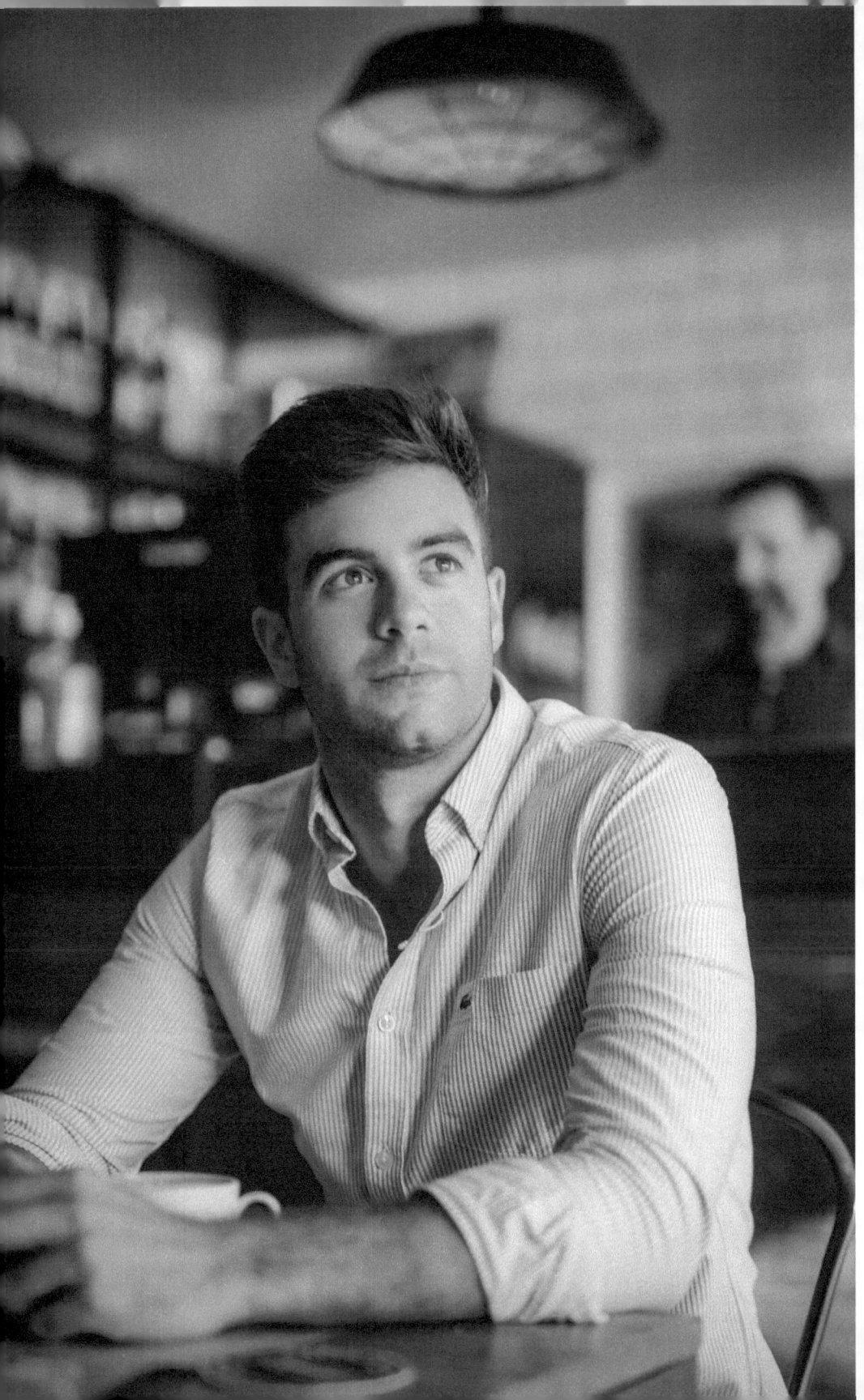

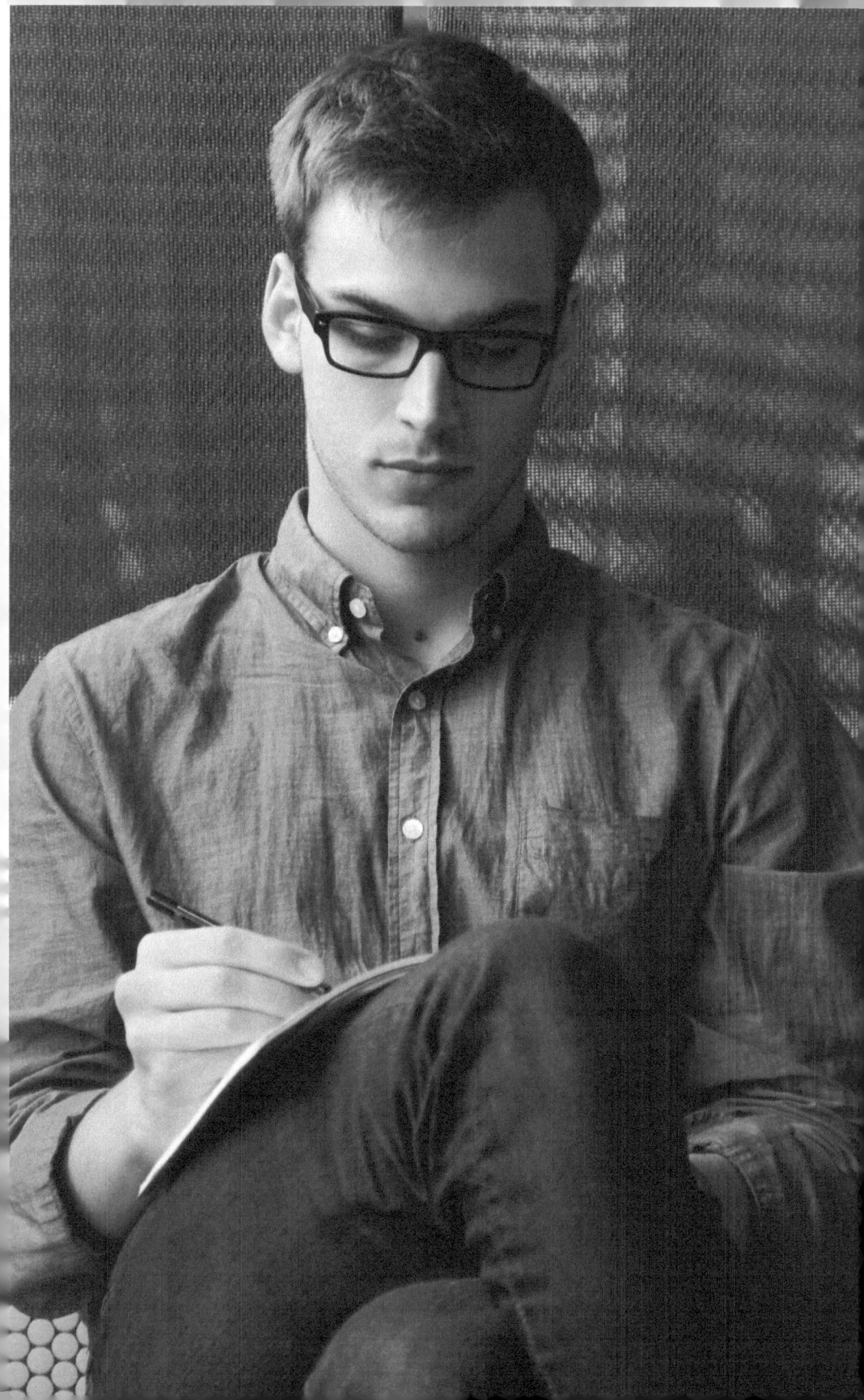

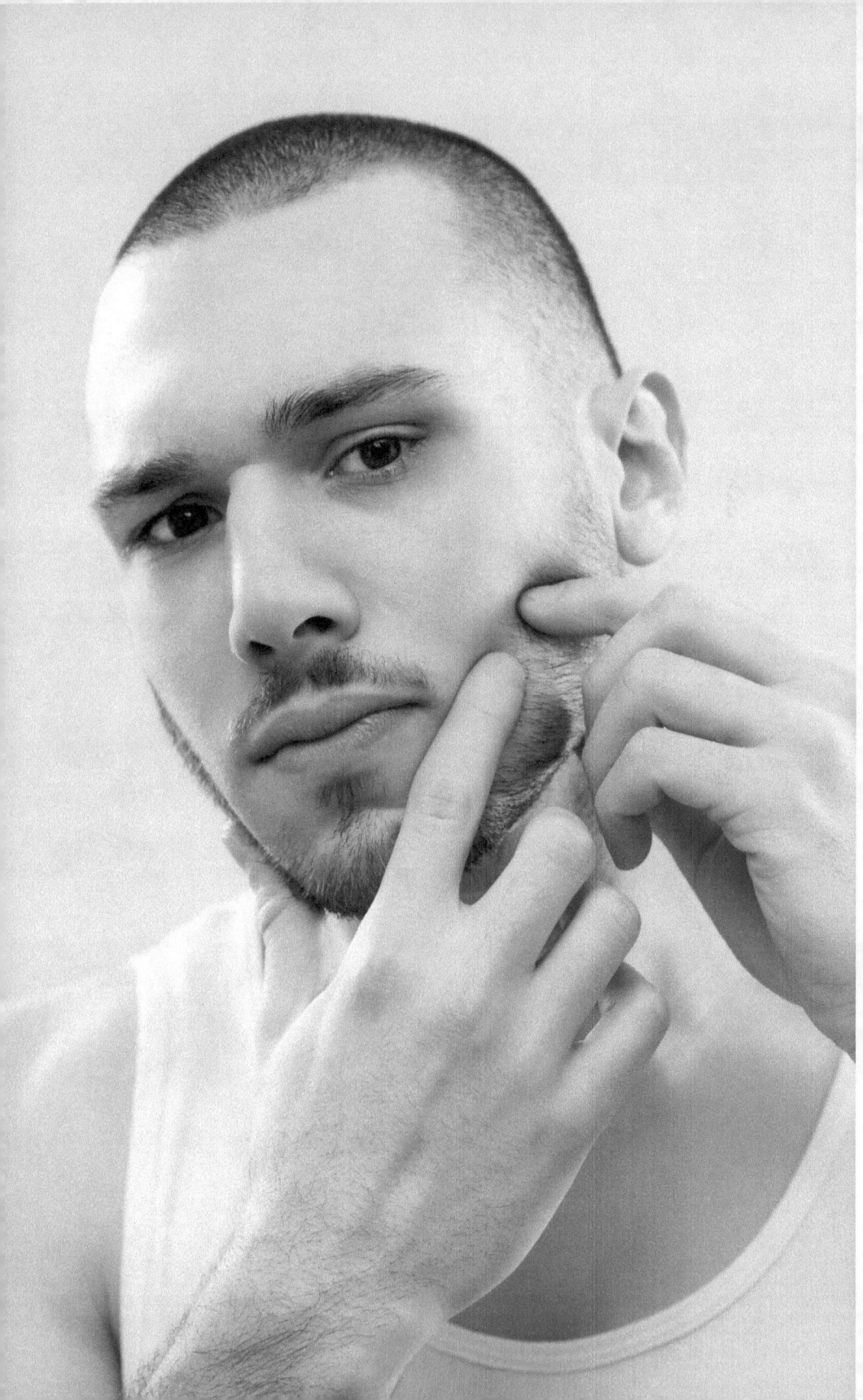

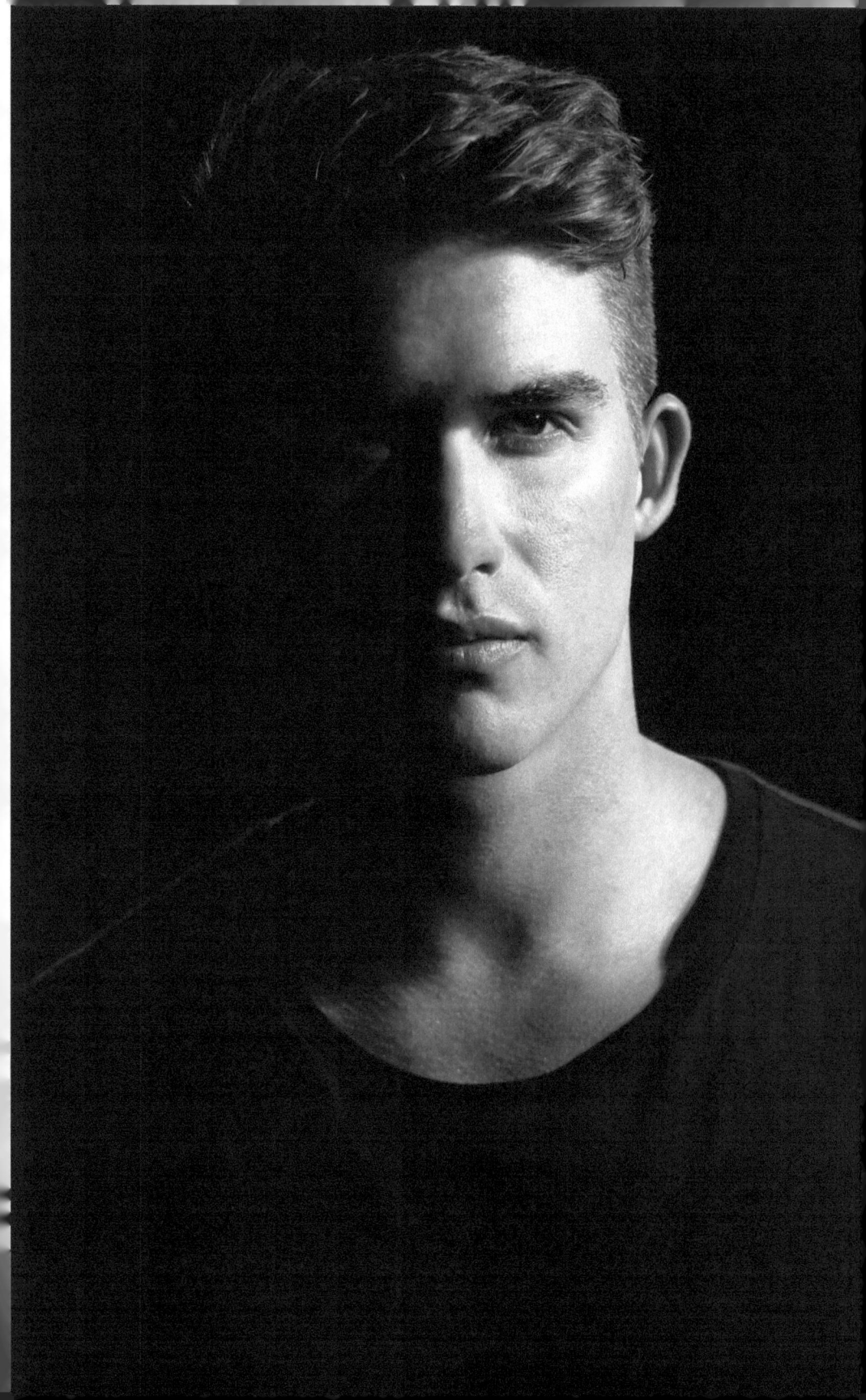

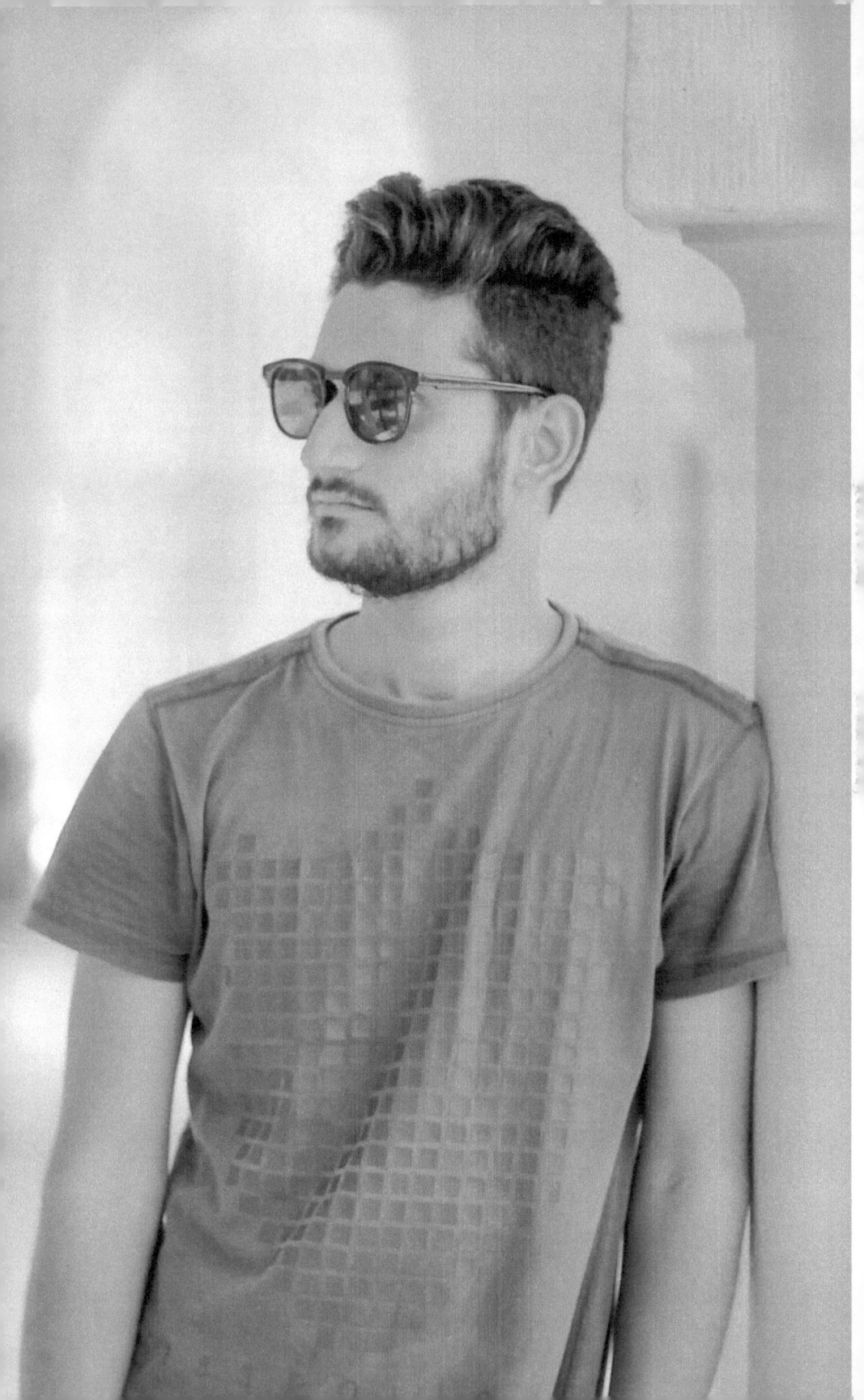

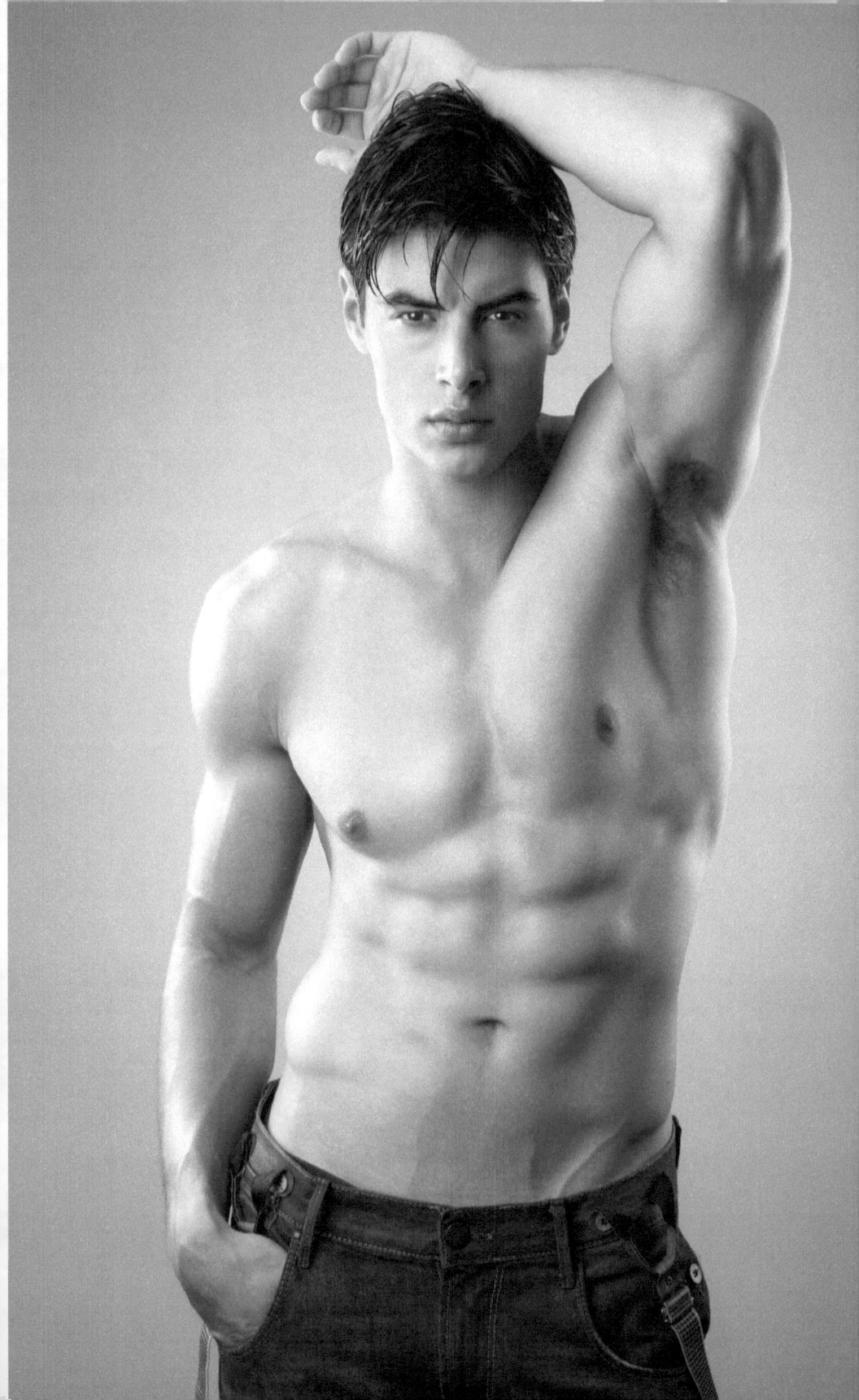

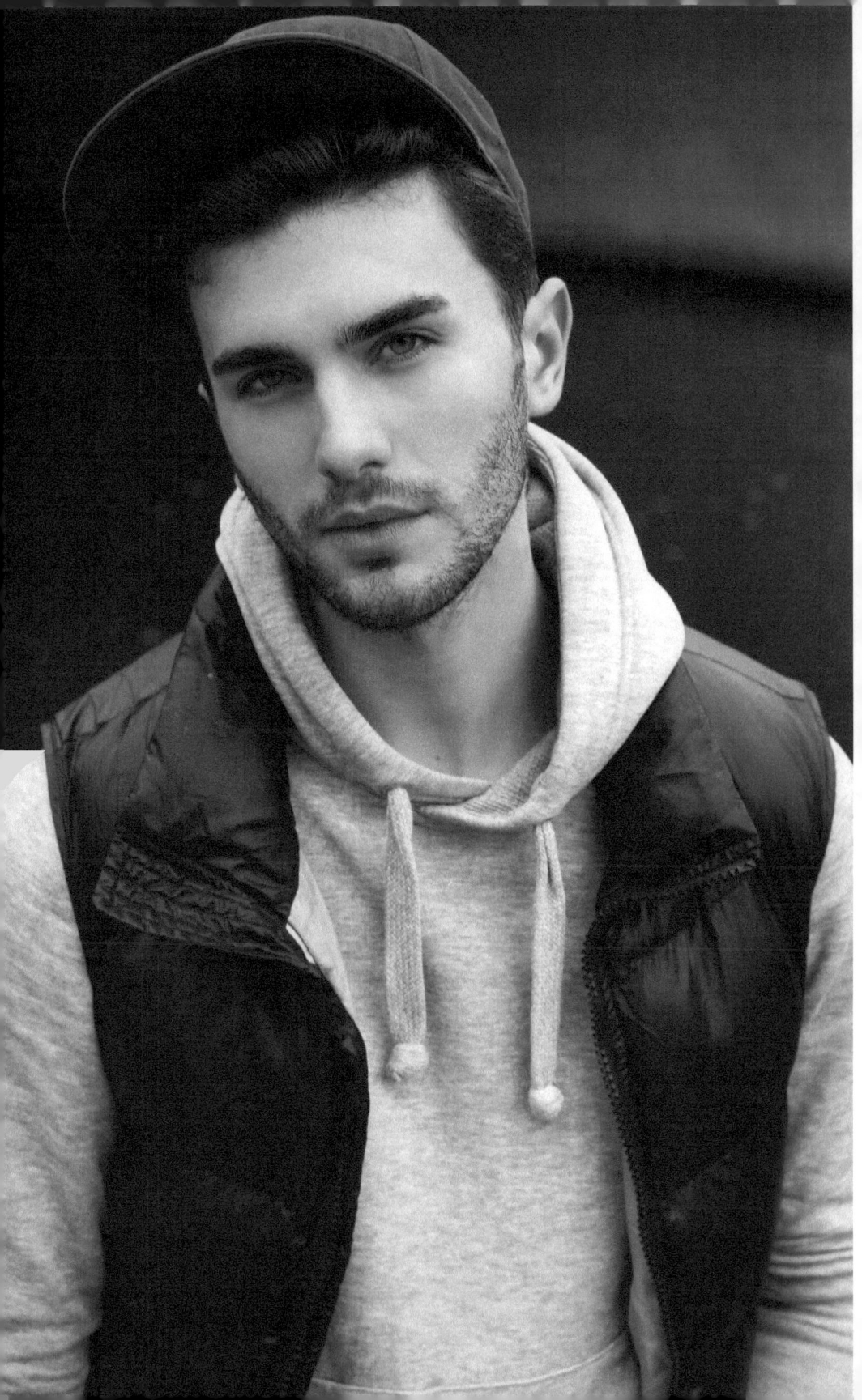

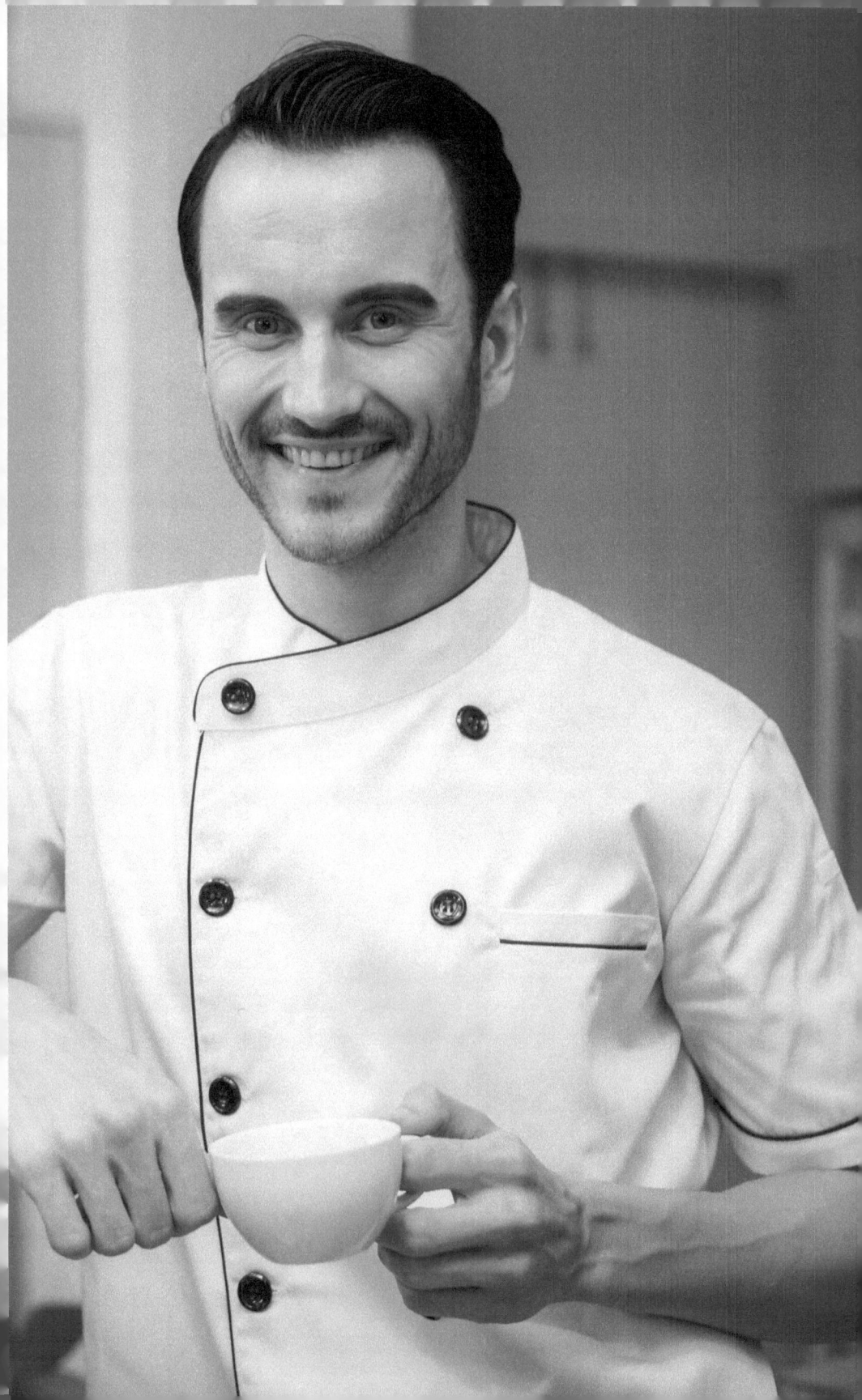

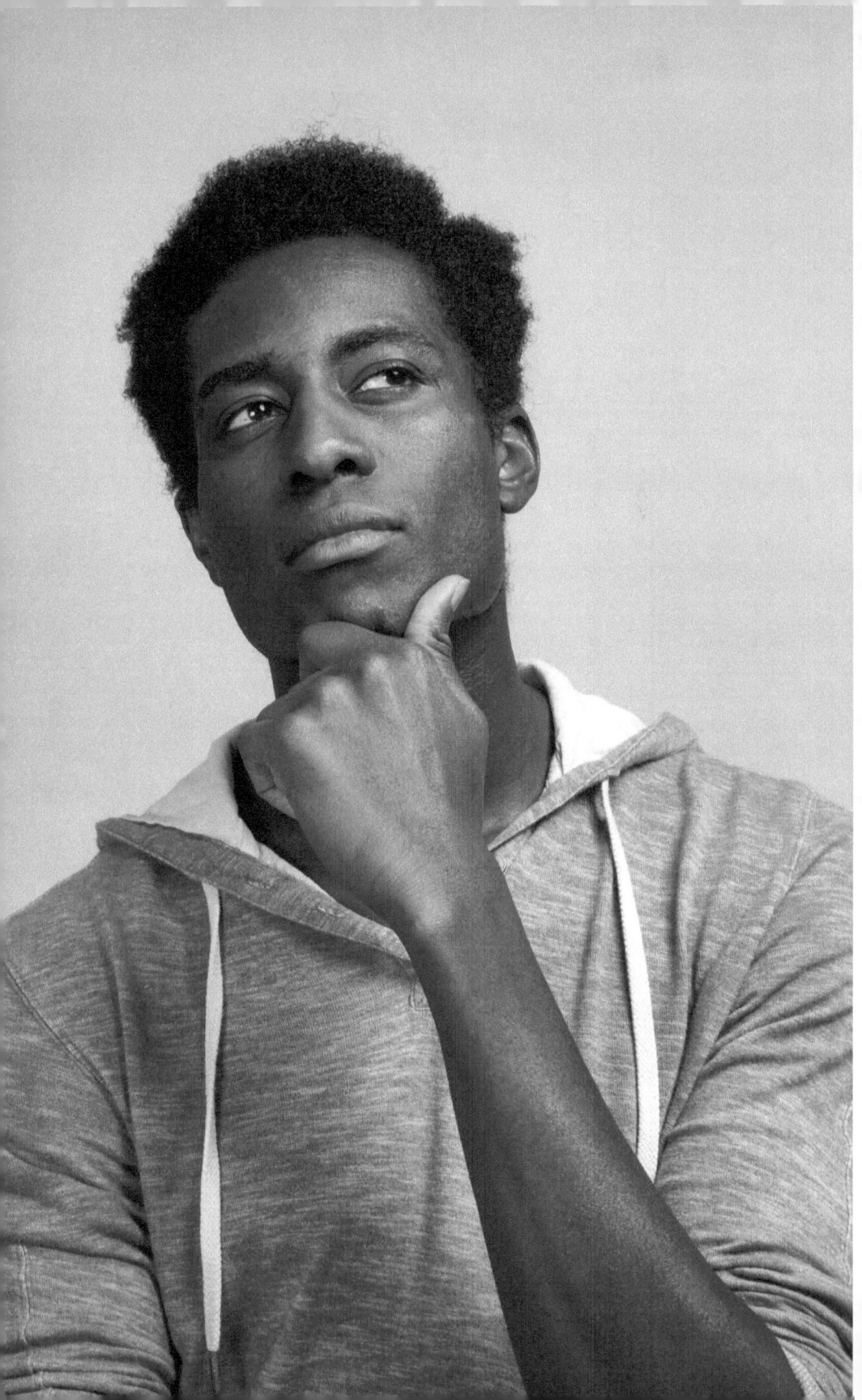

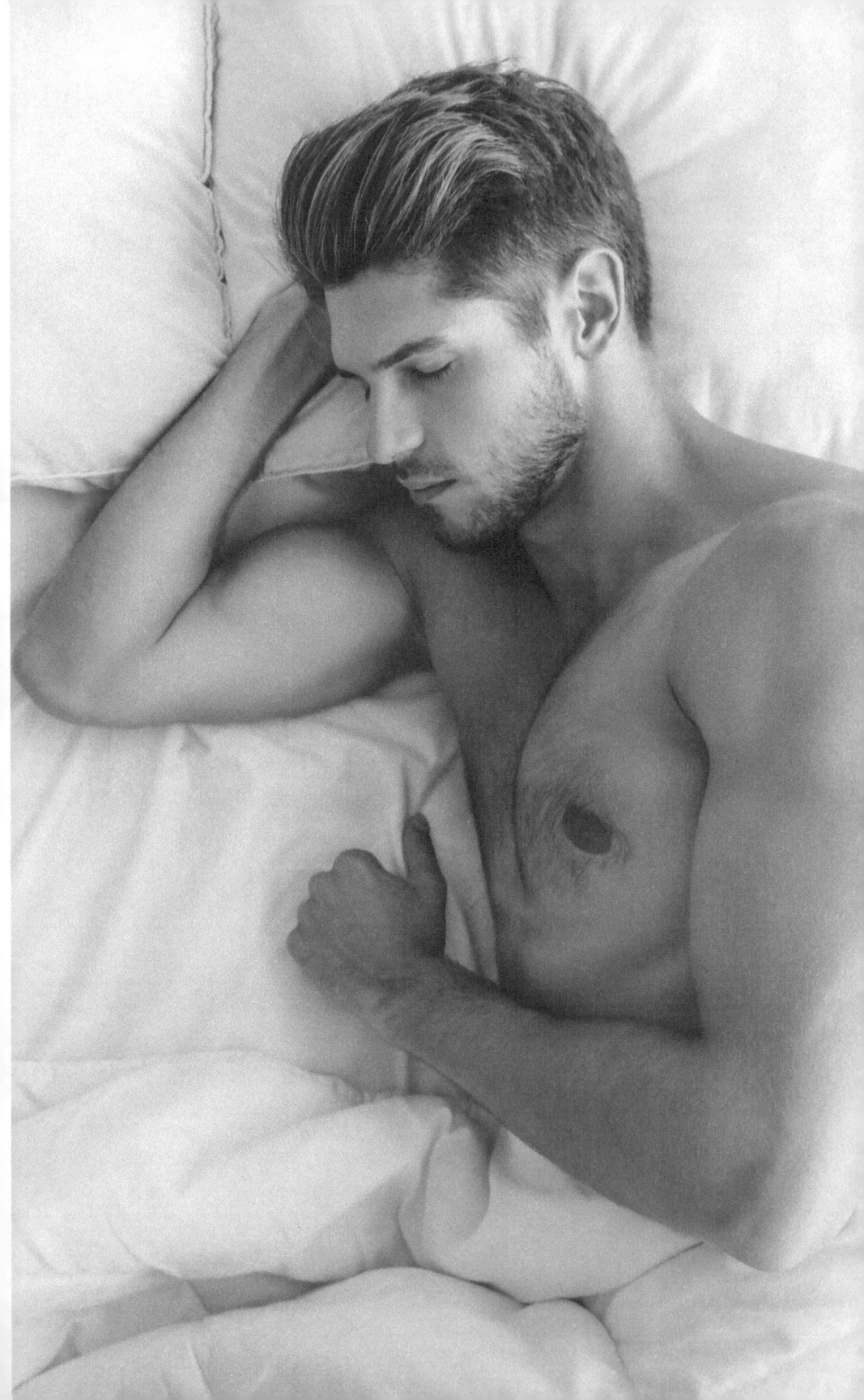

"I have always believed that your face is a mirror to your nature."

Sridevi

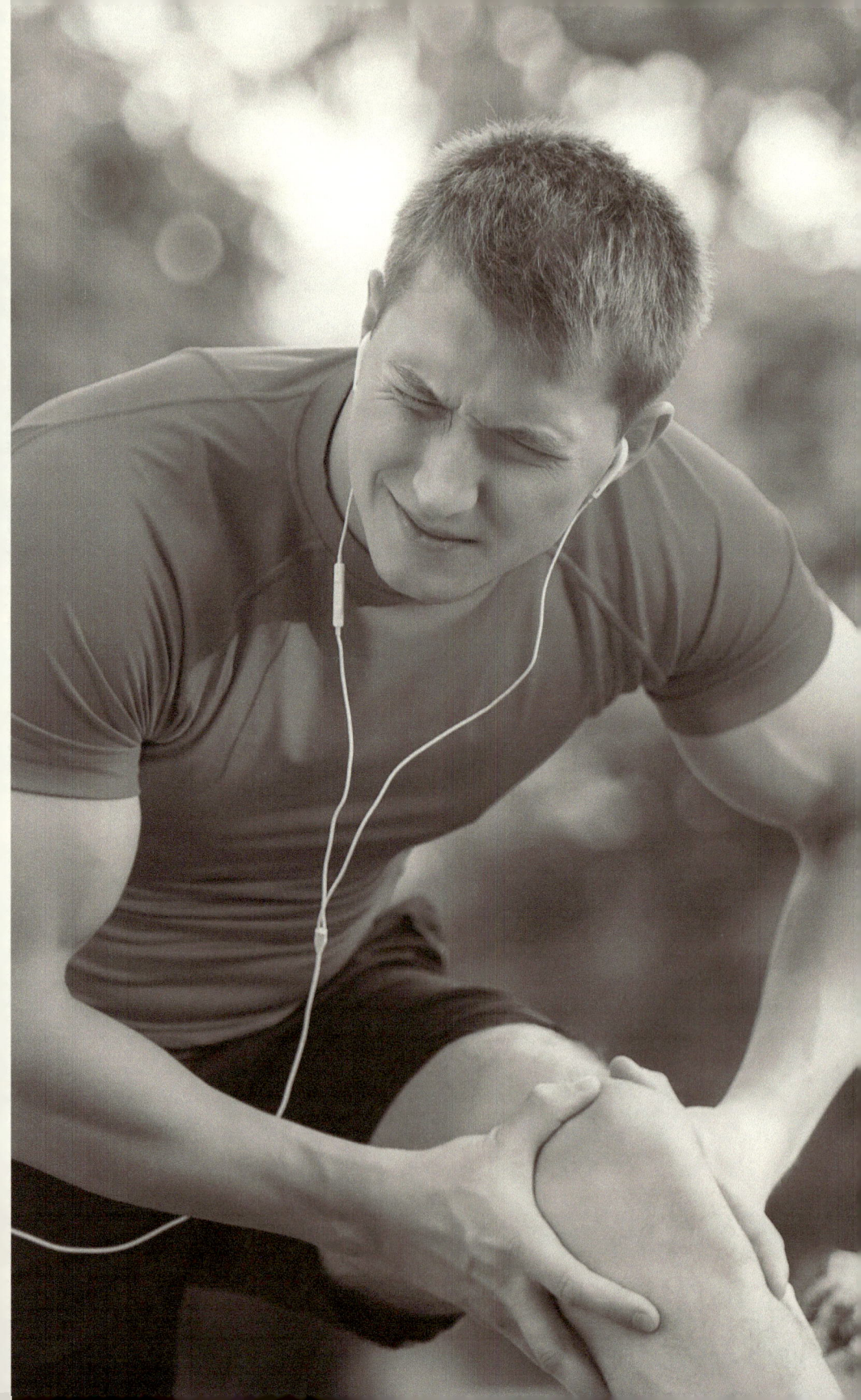

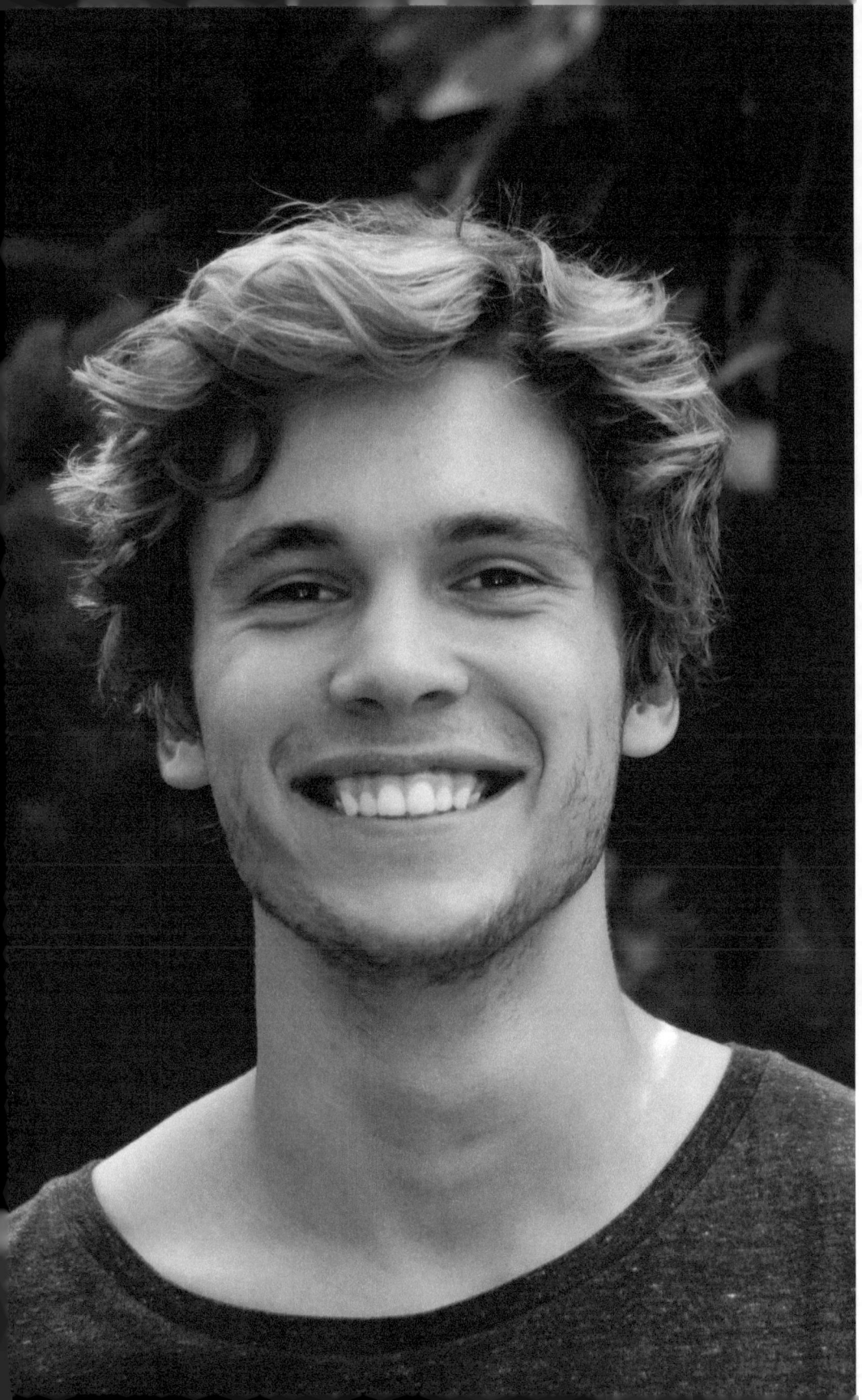

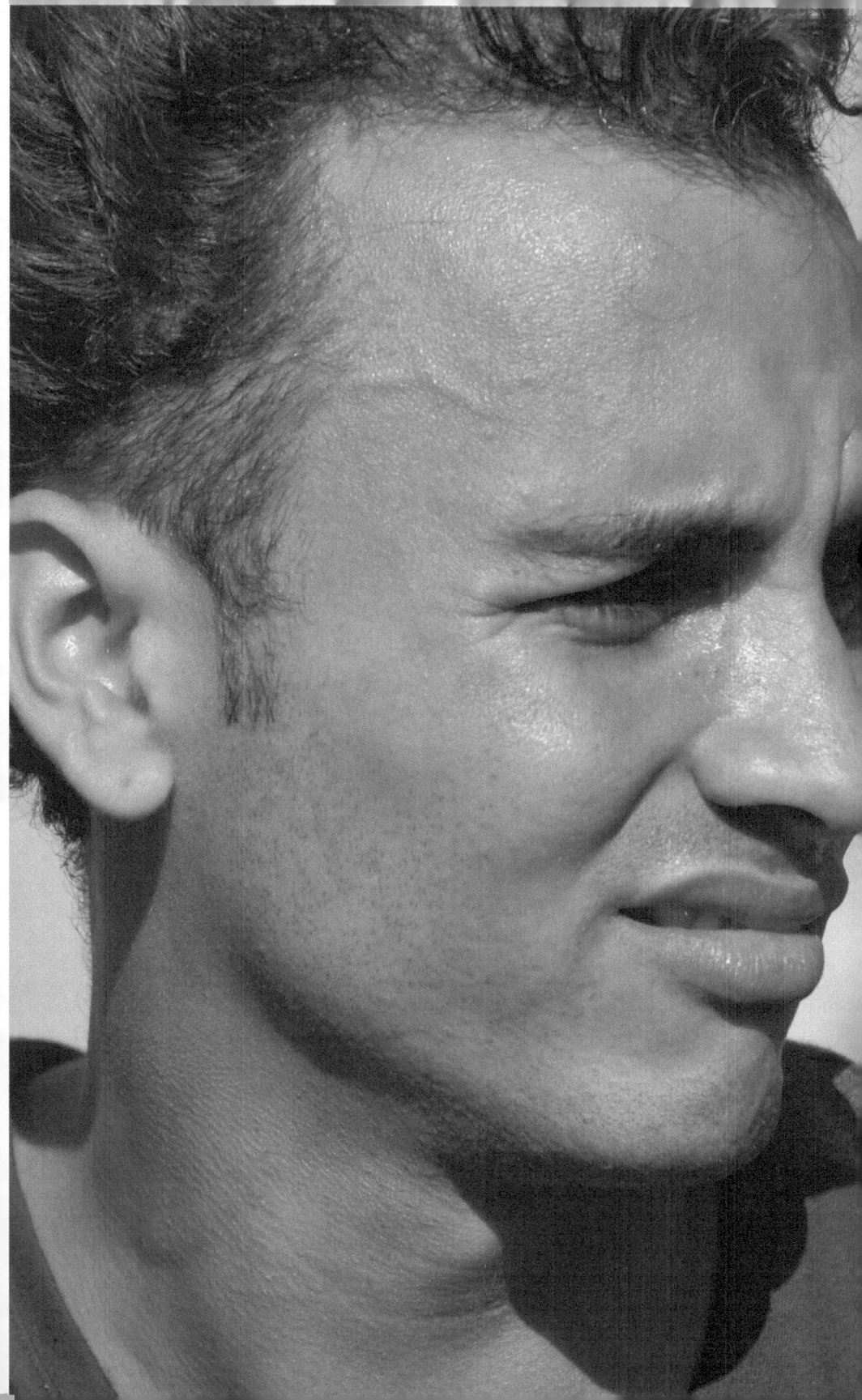

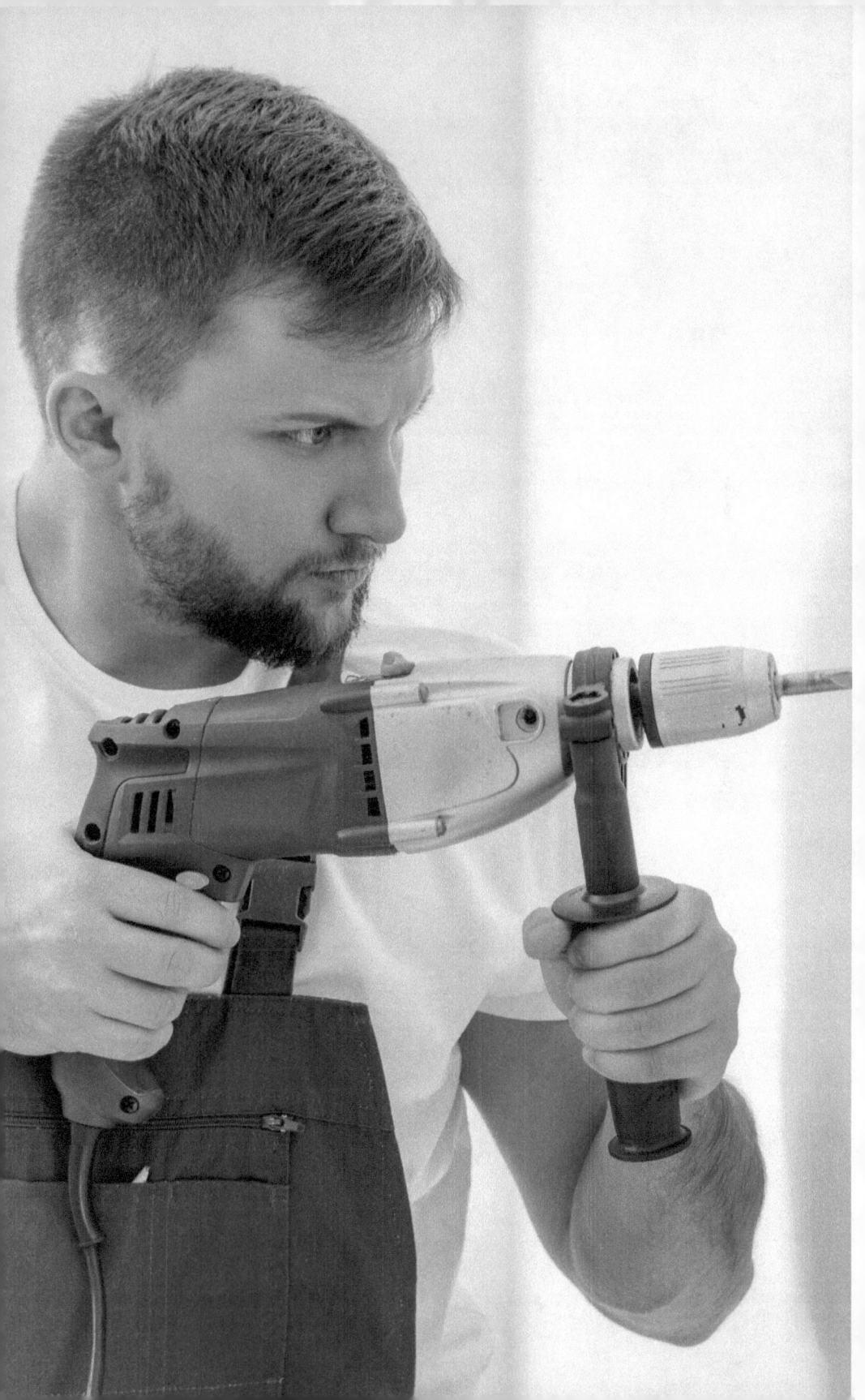

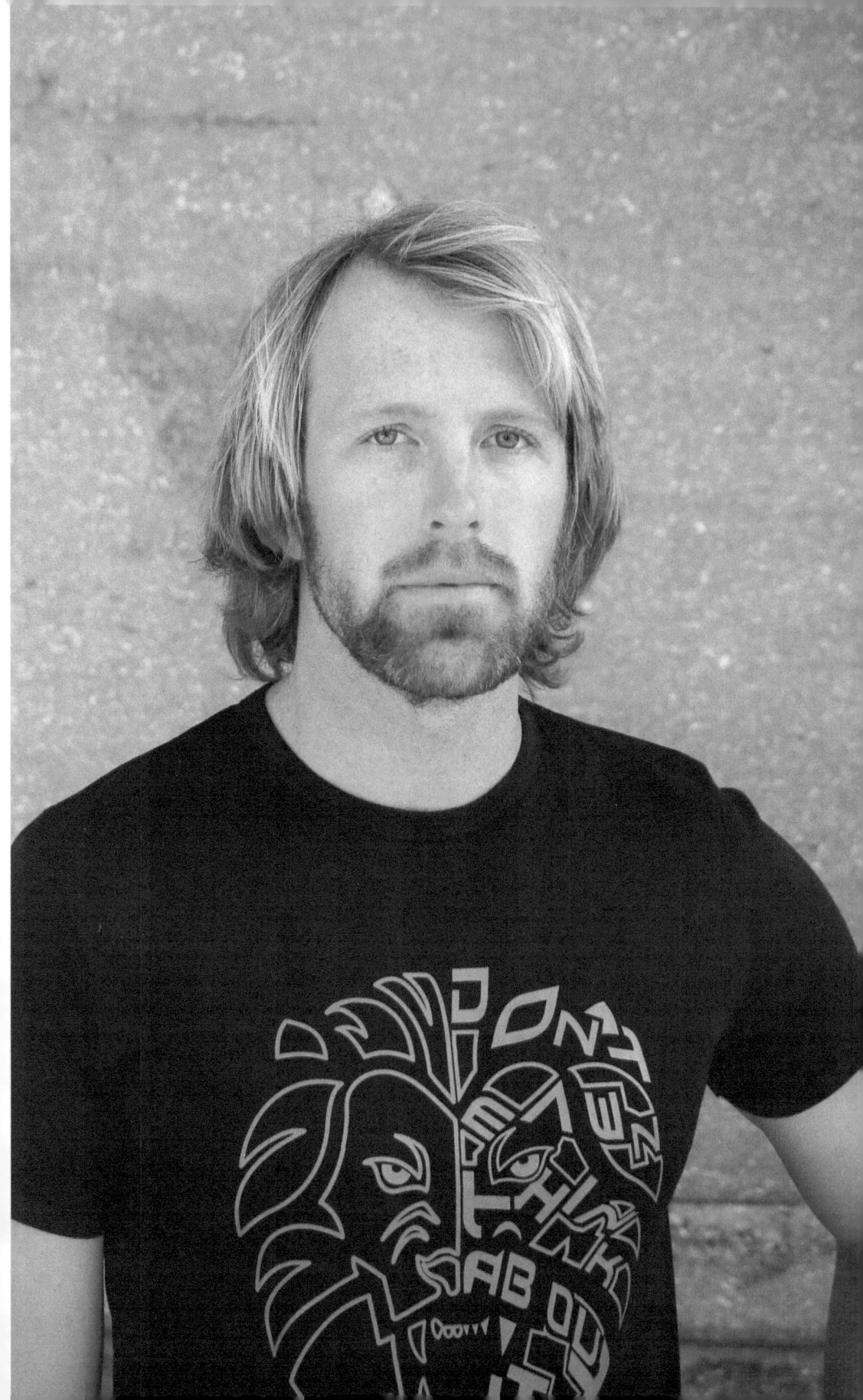

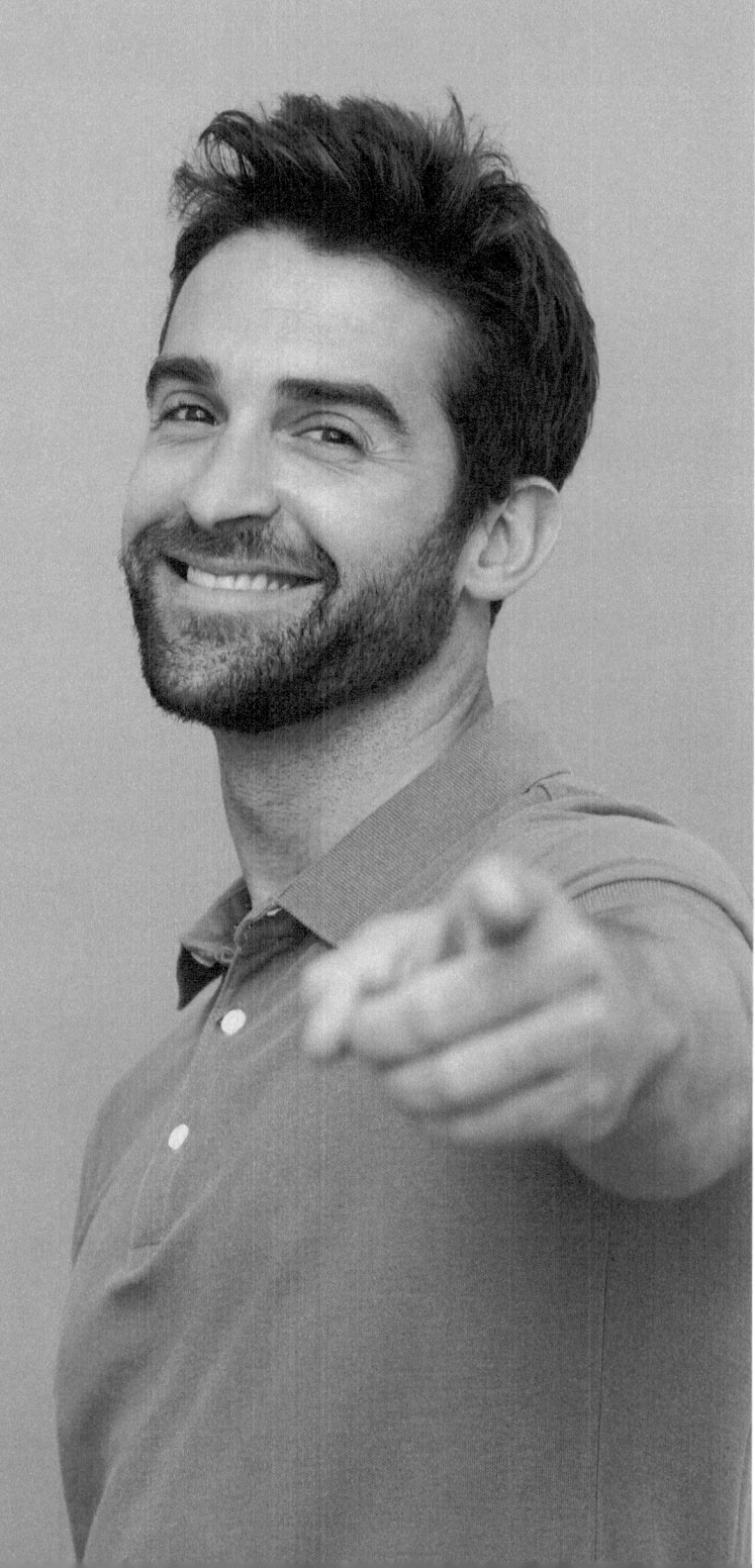

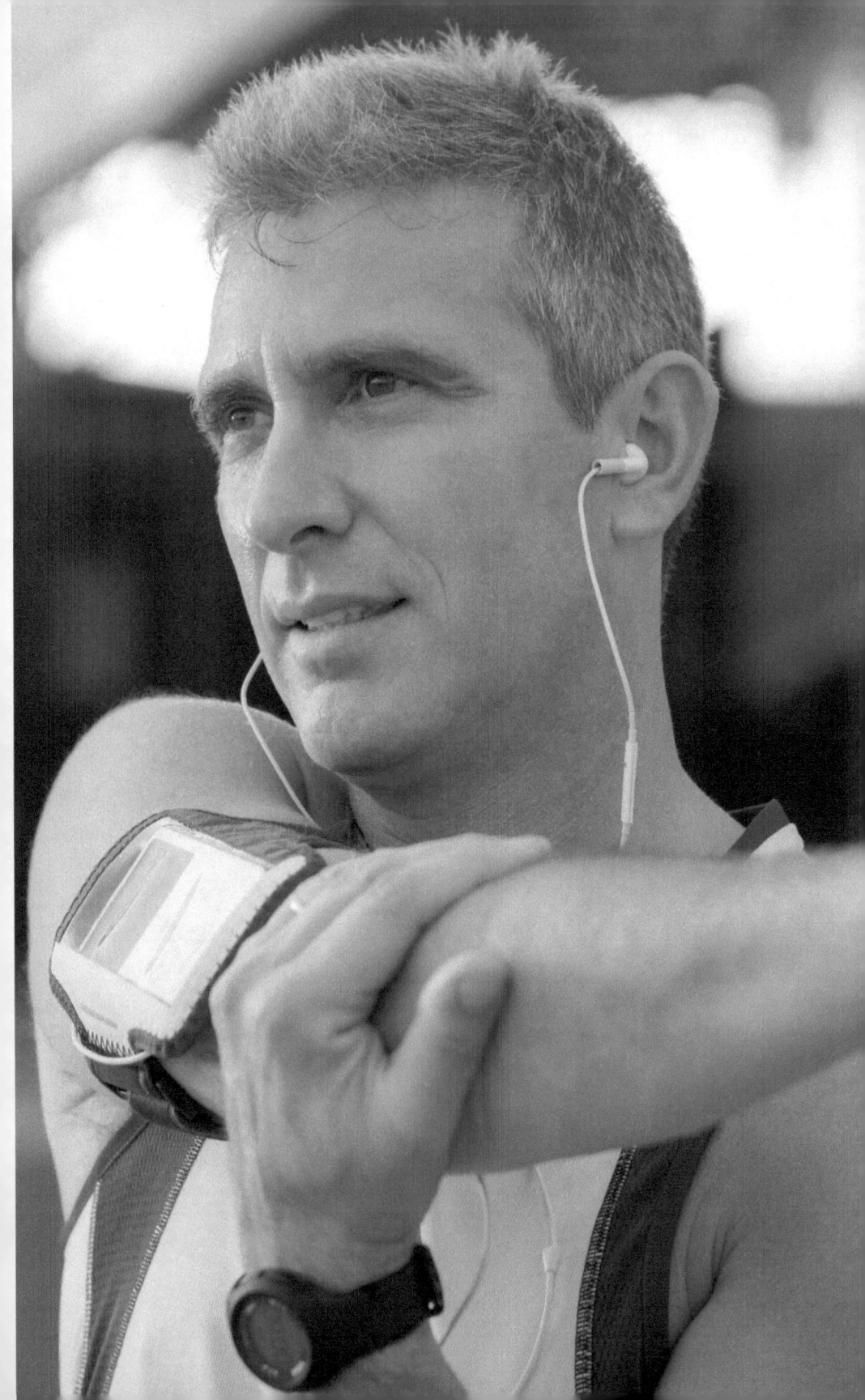

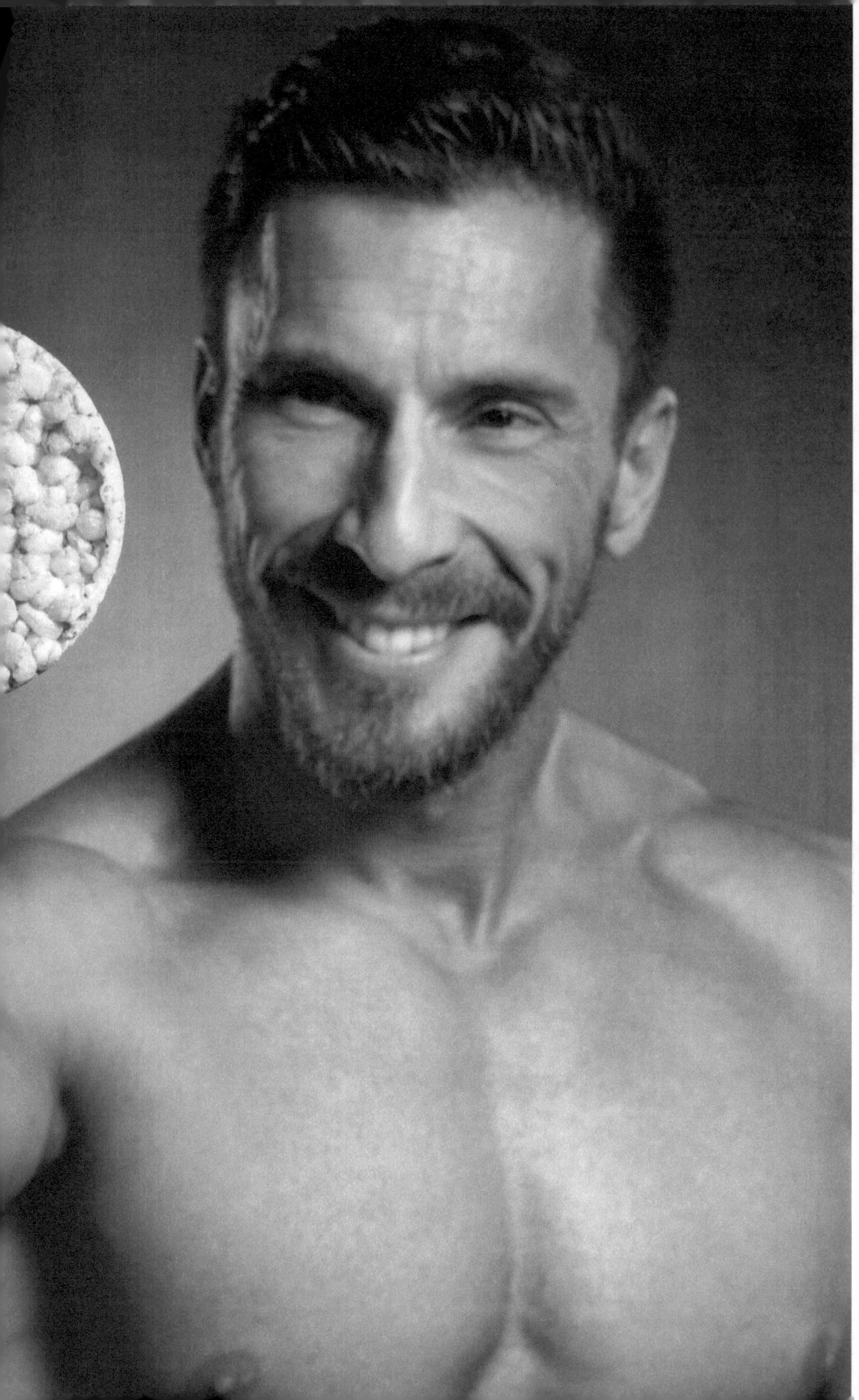

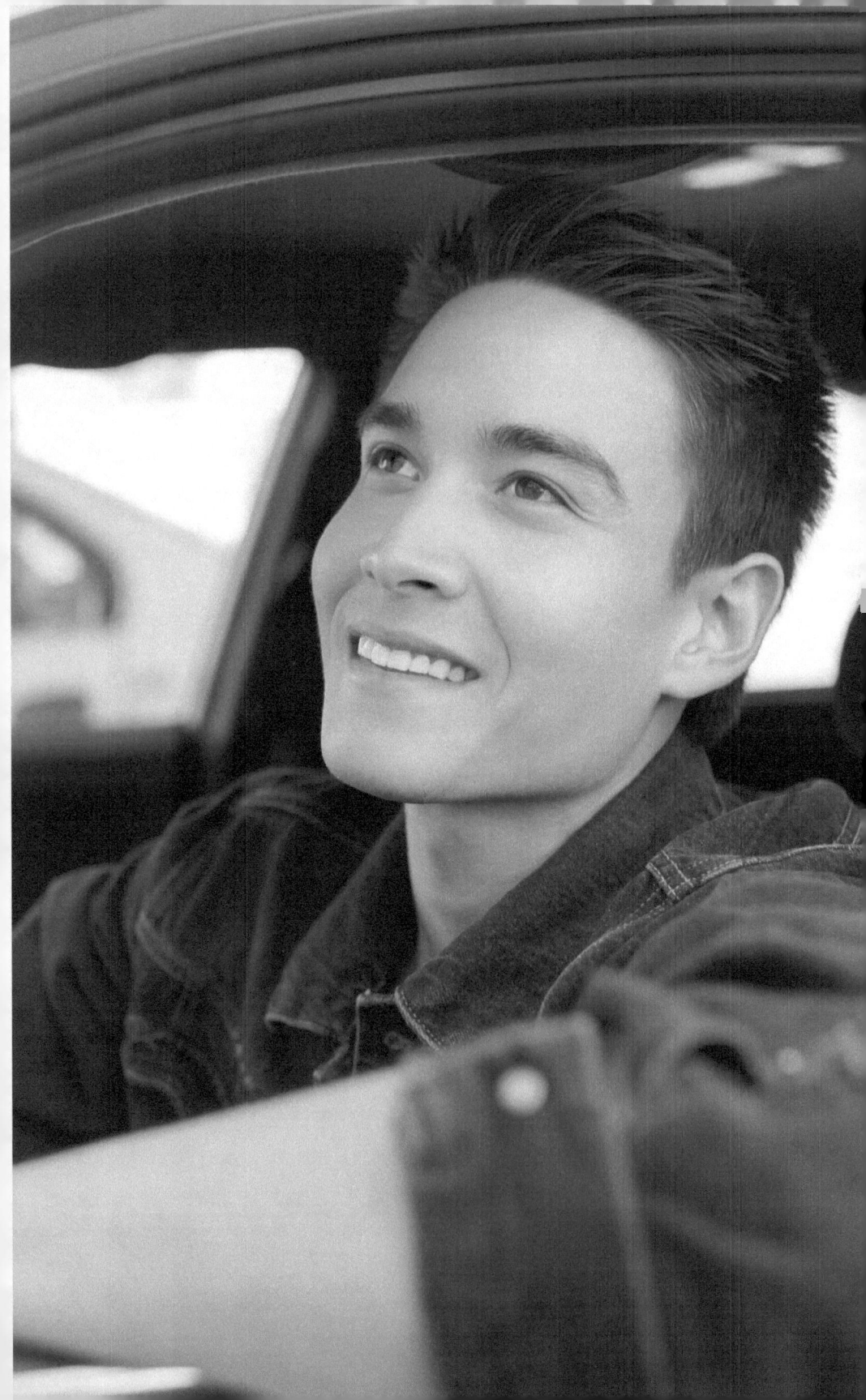

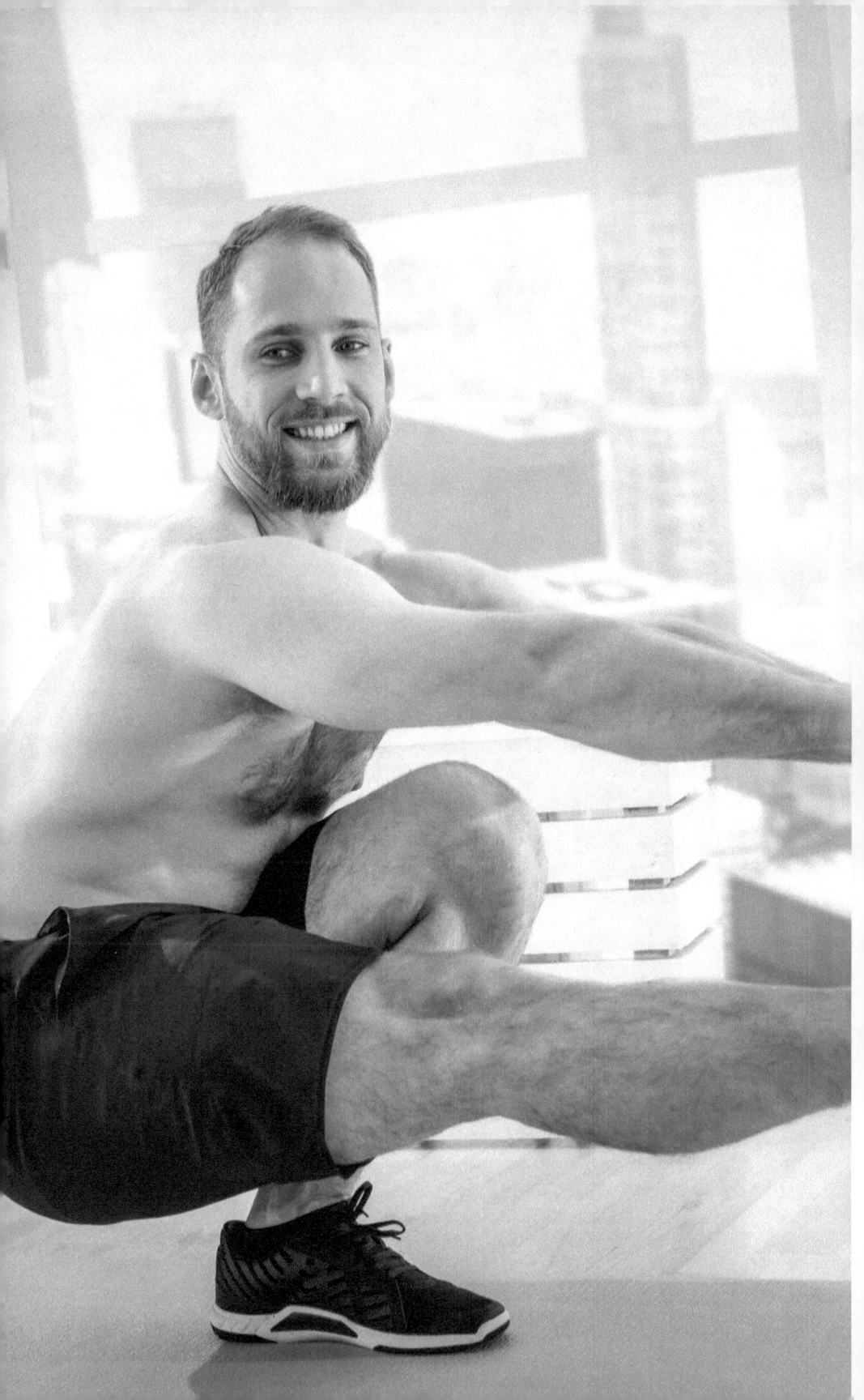

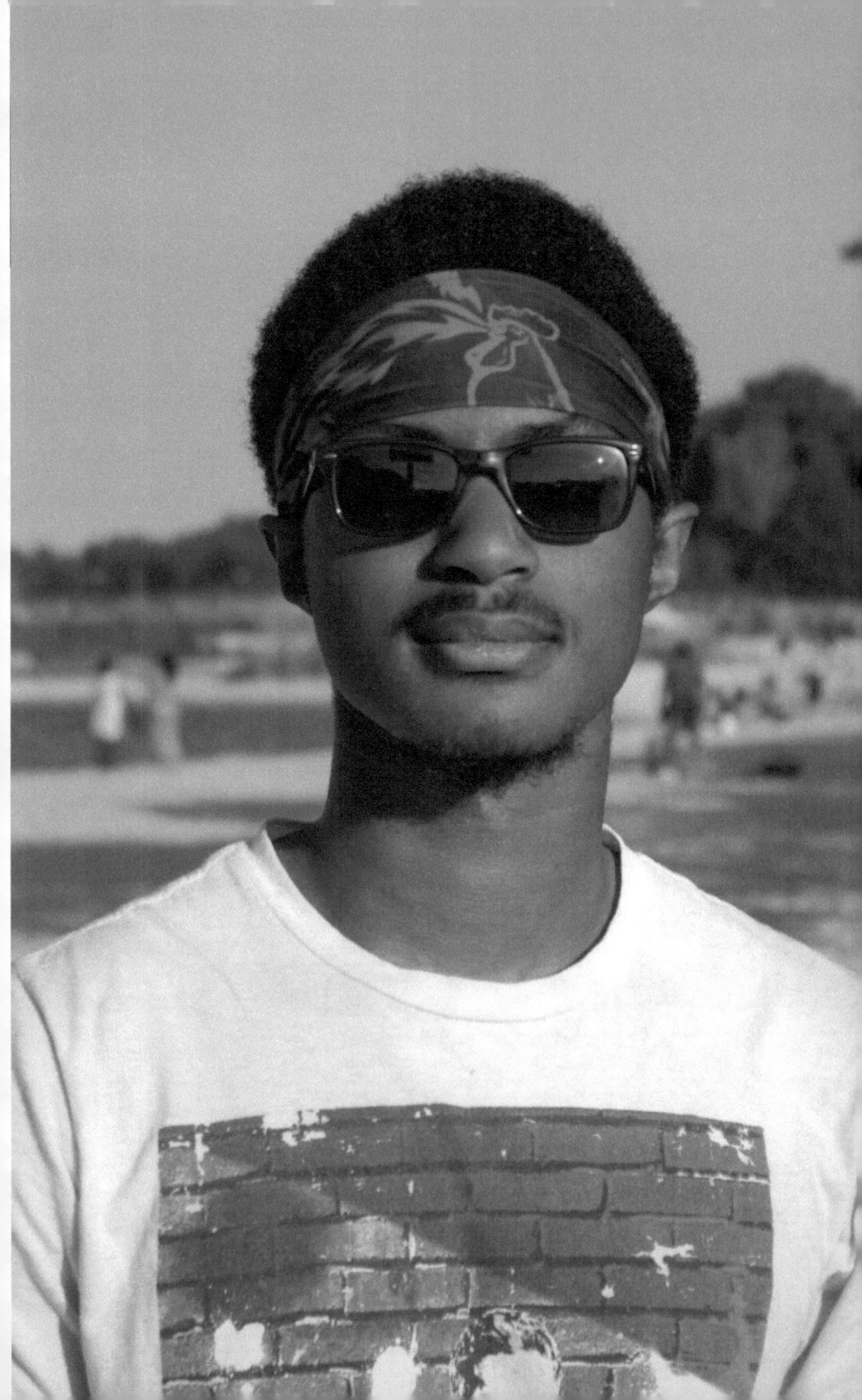

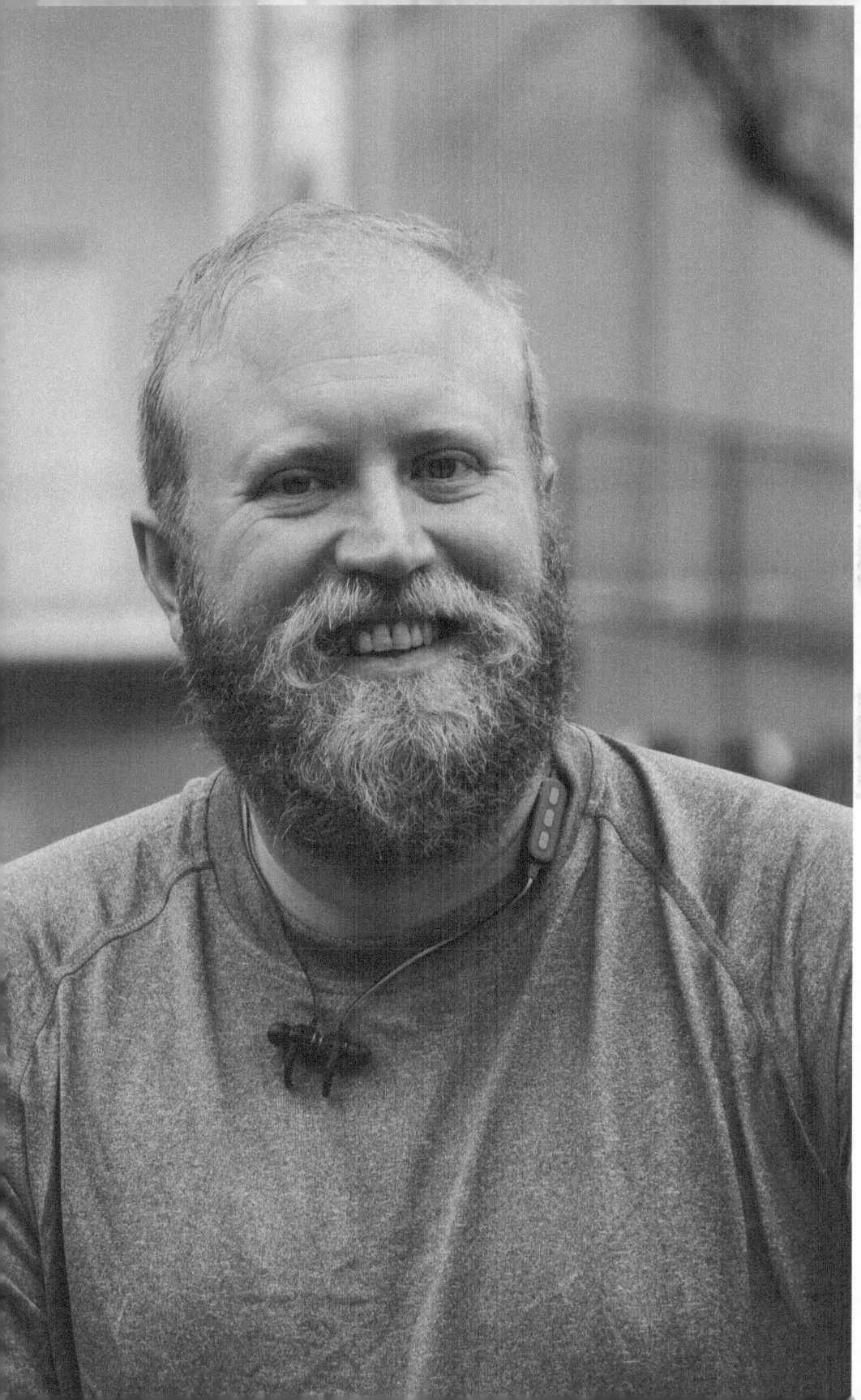

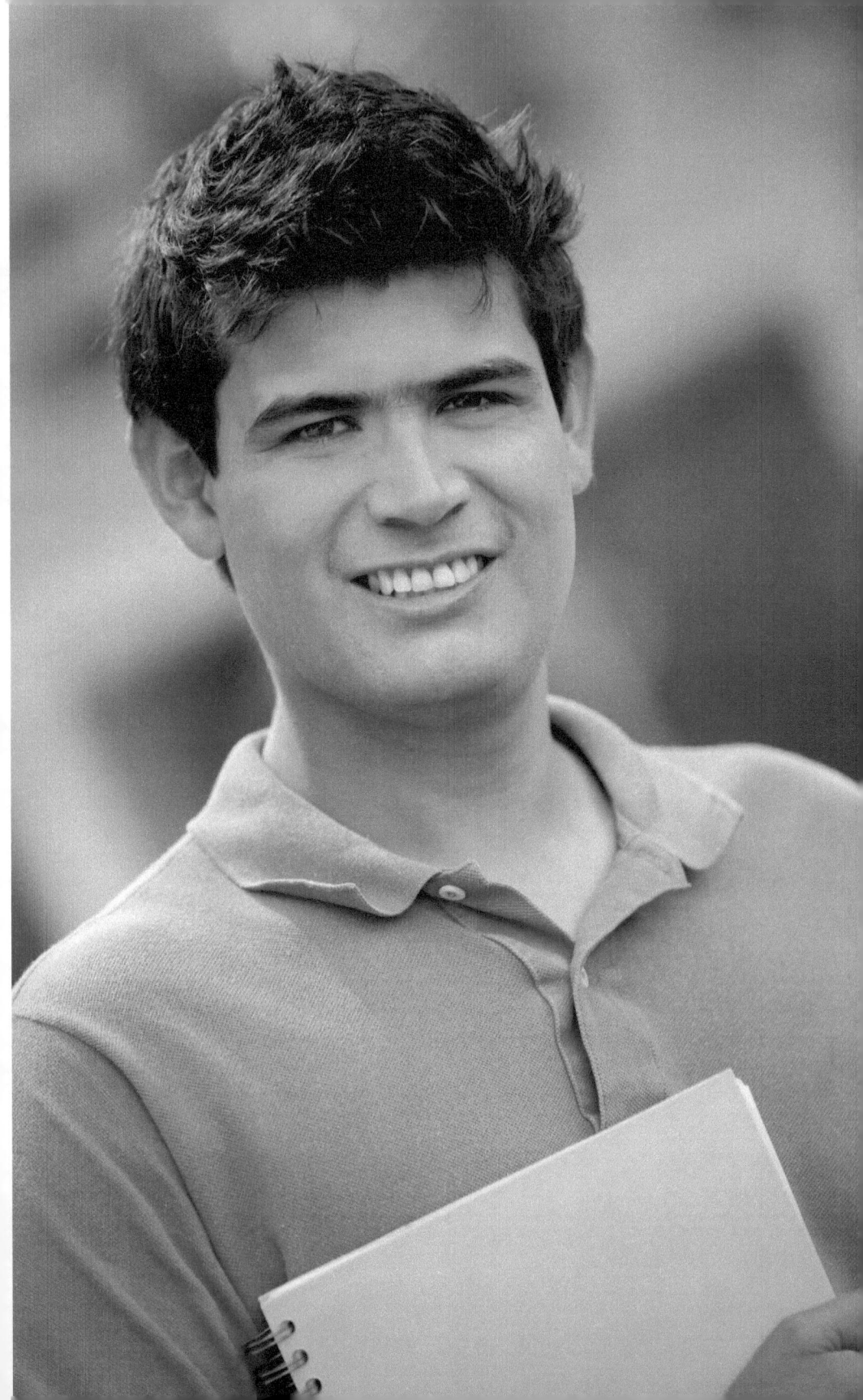

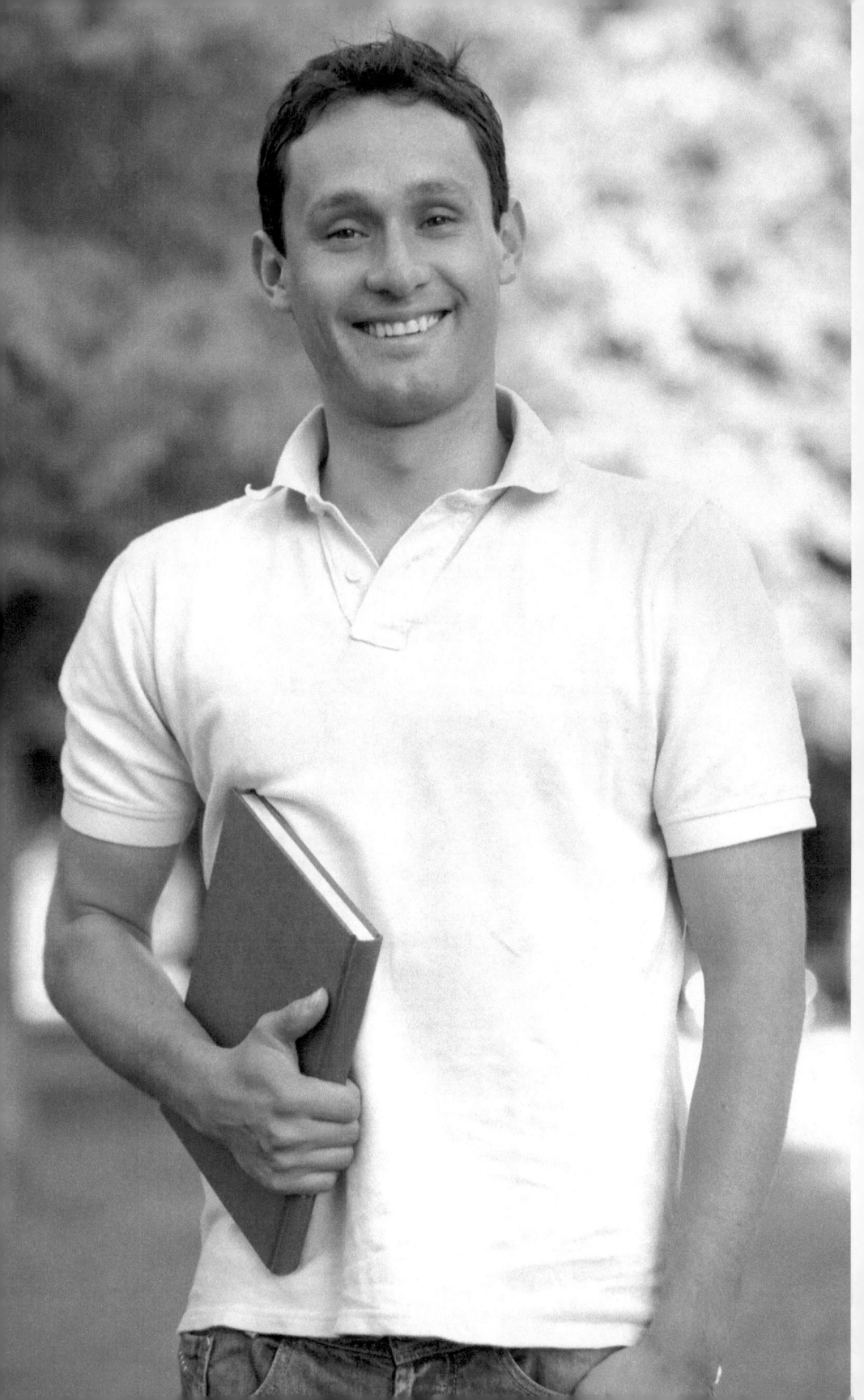

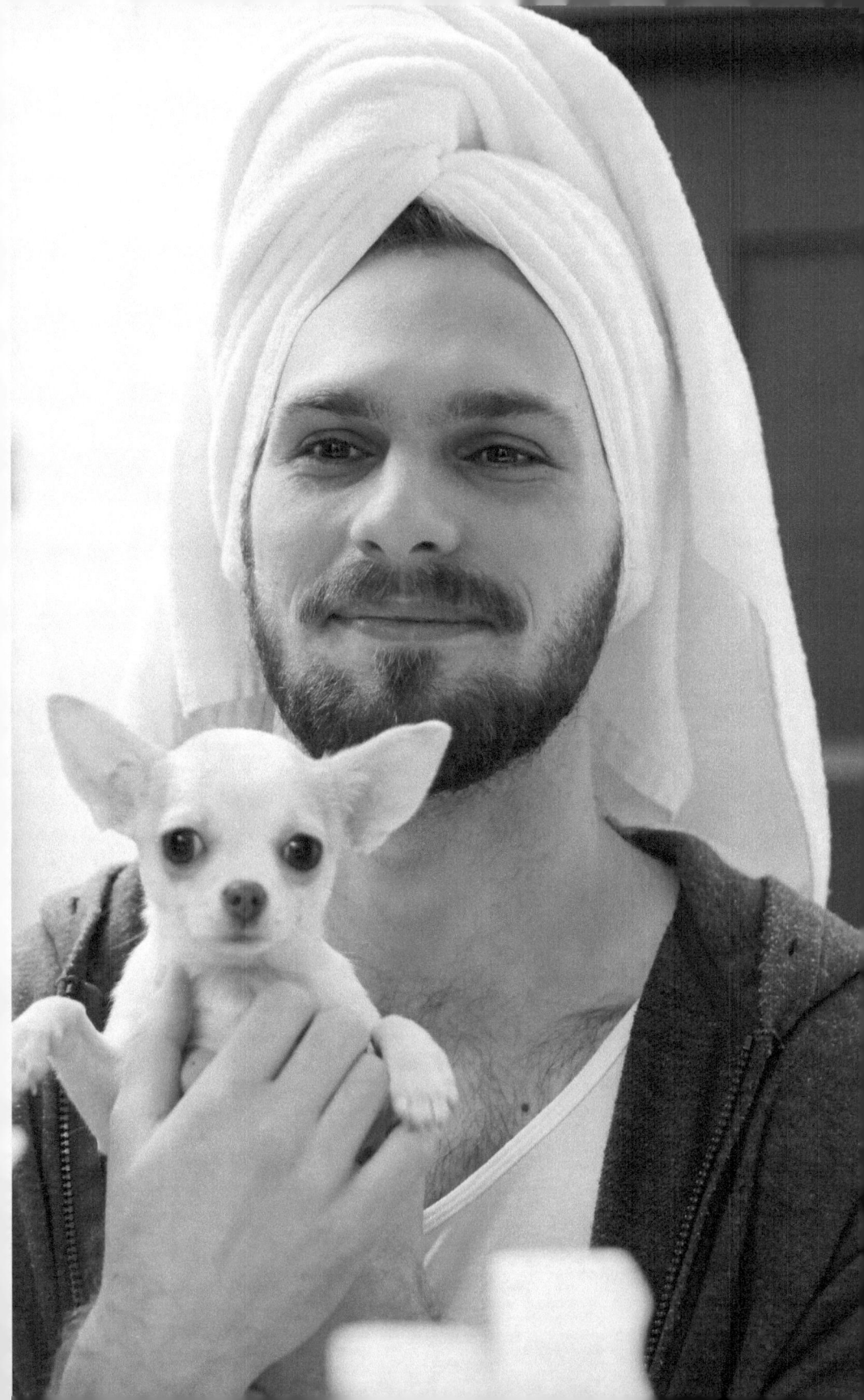

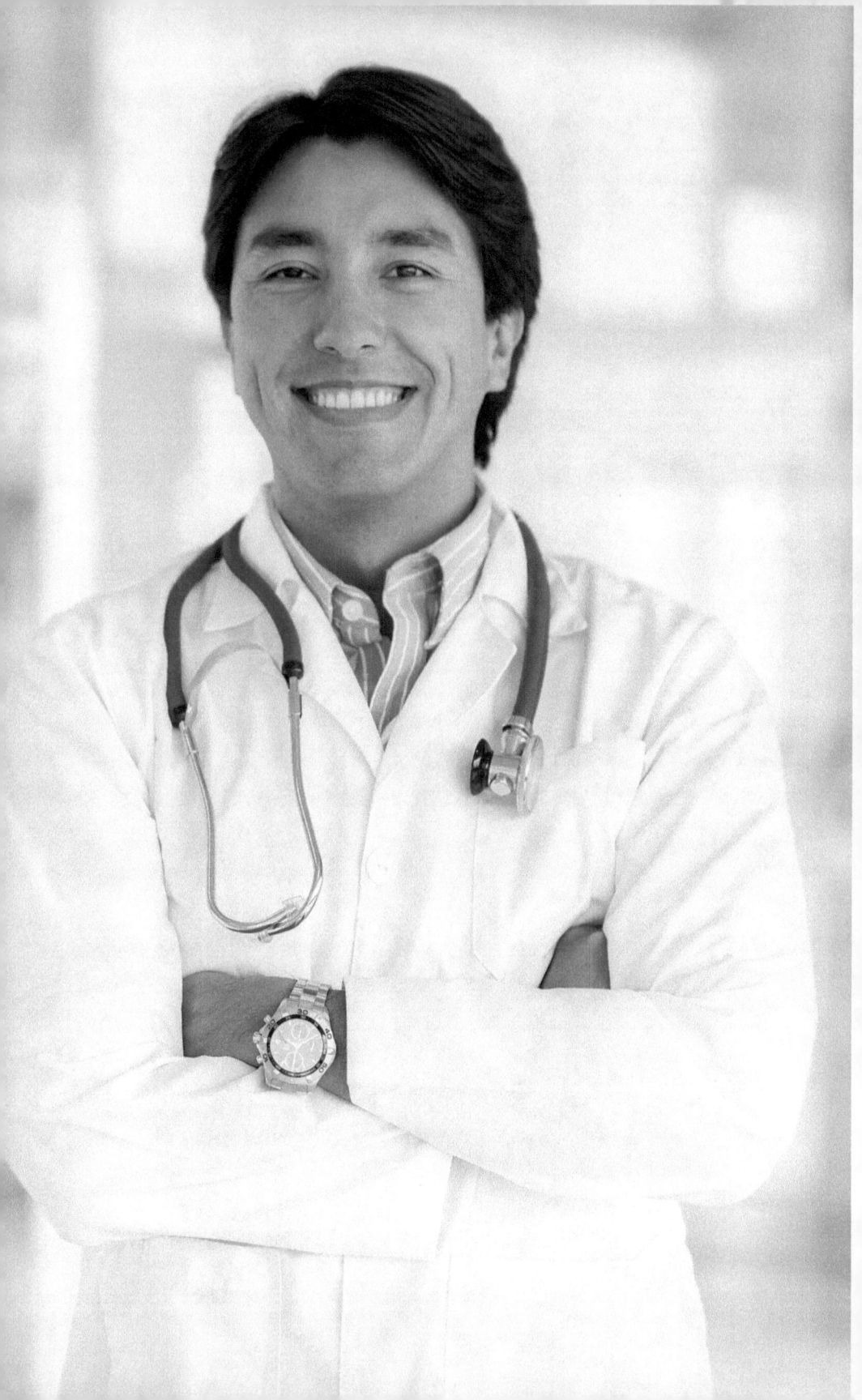

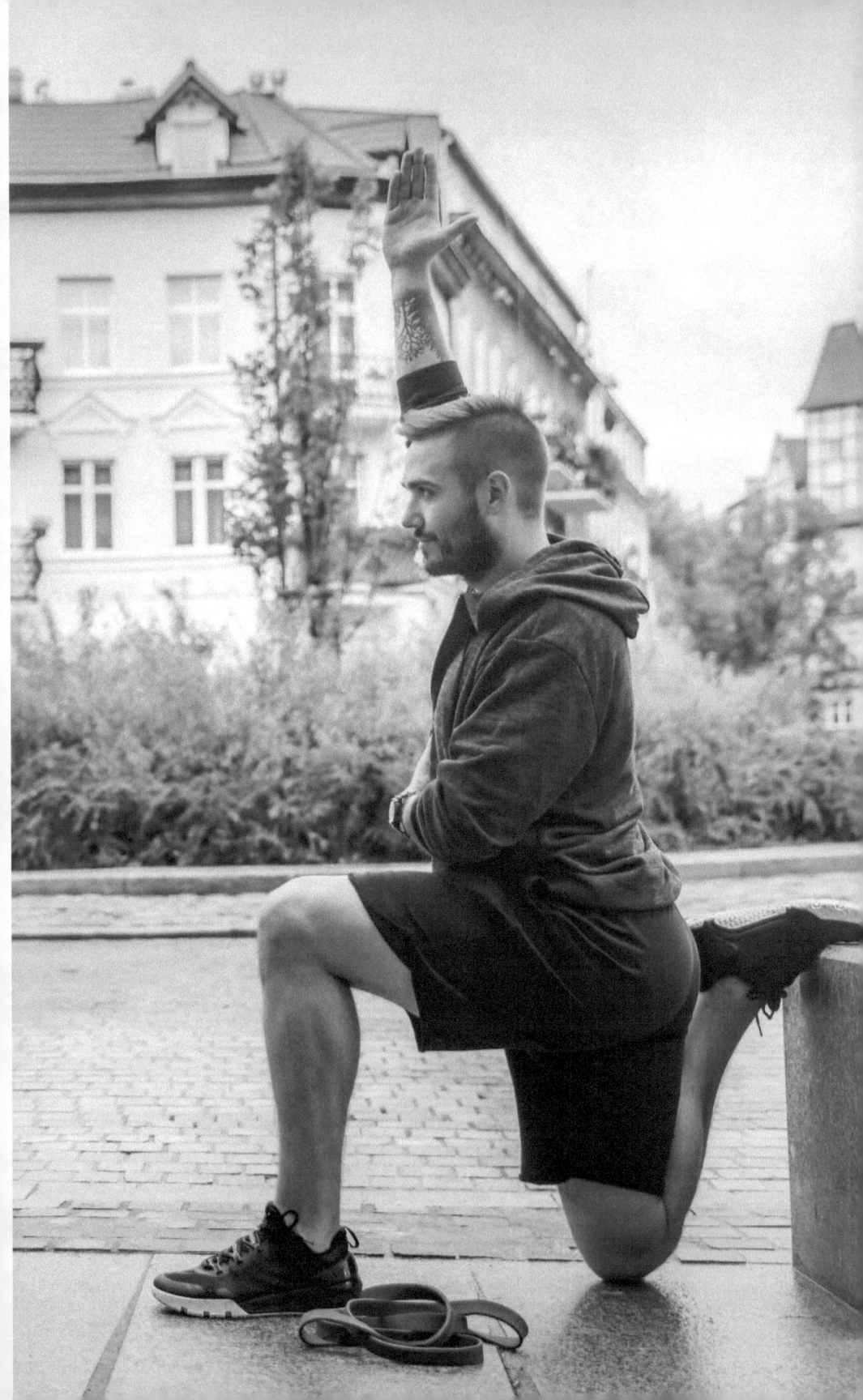

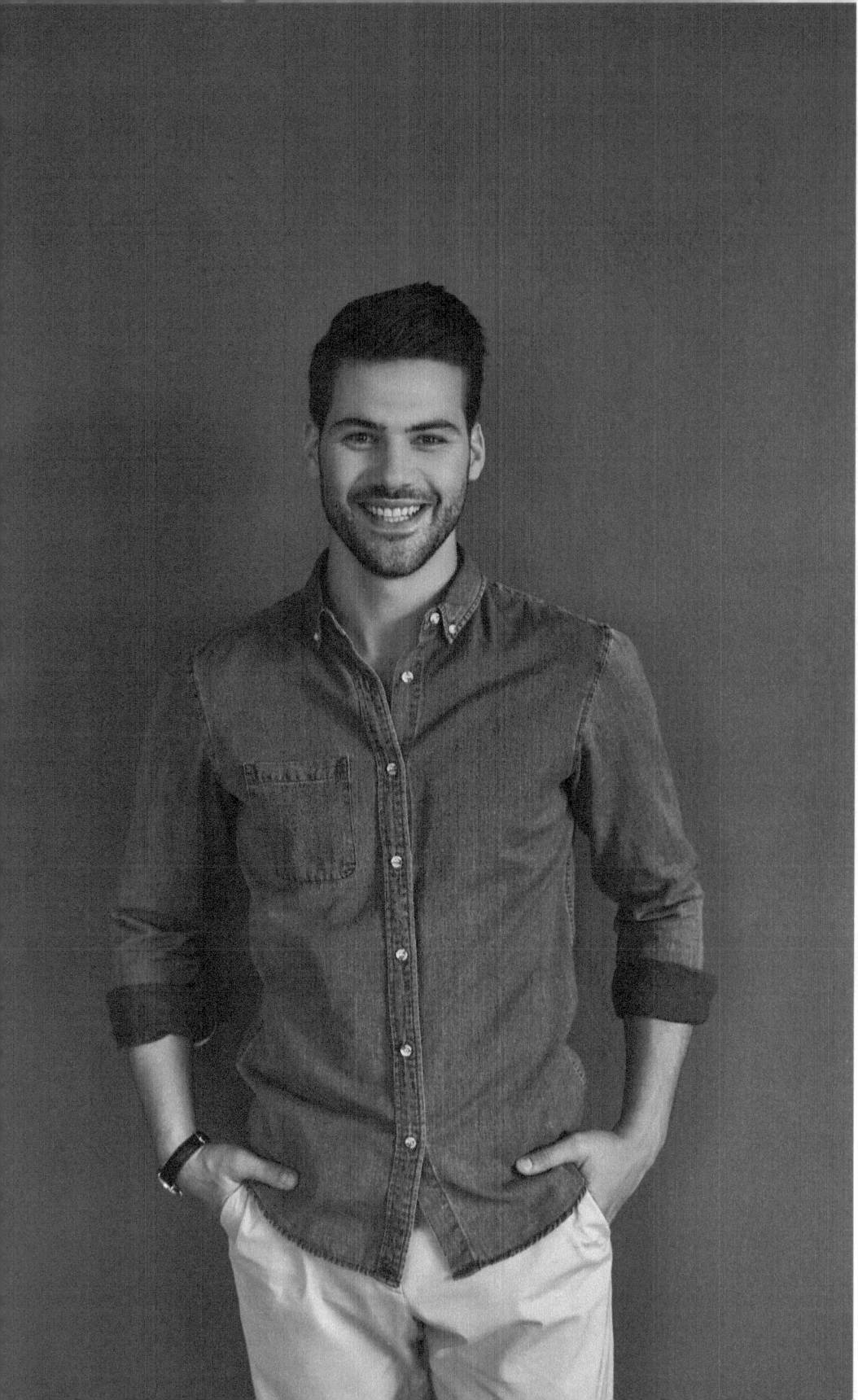

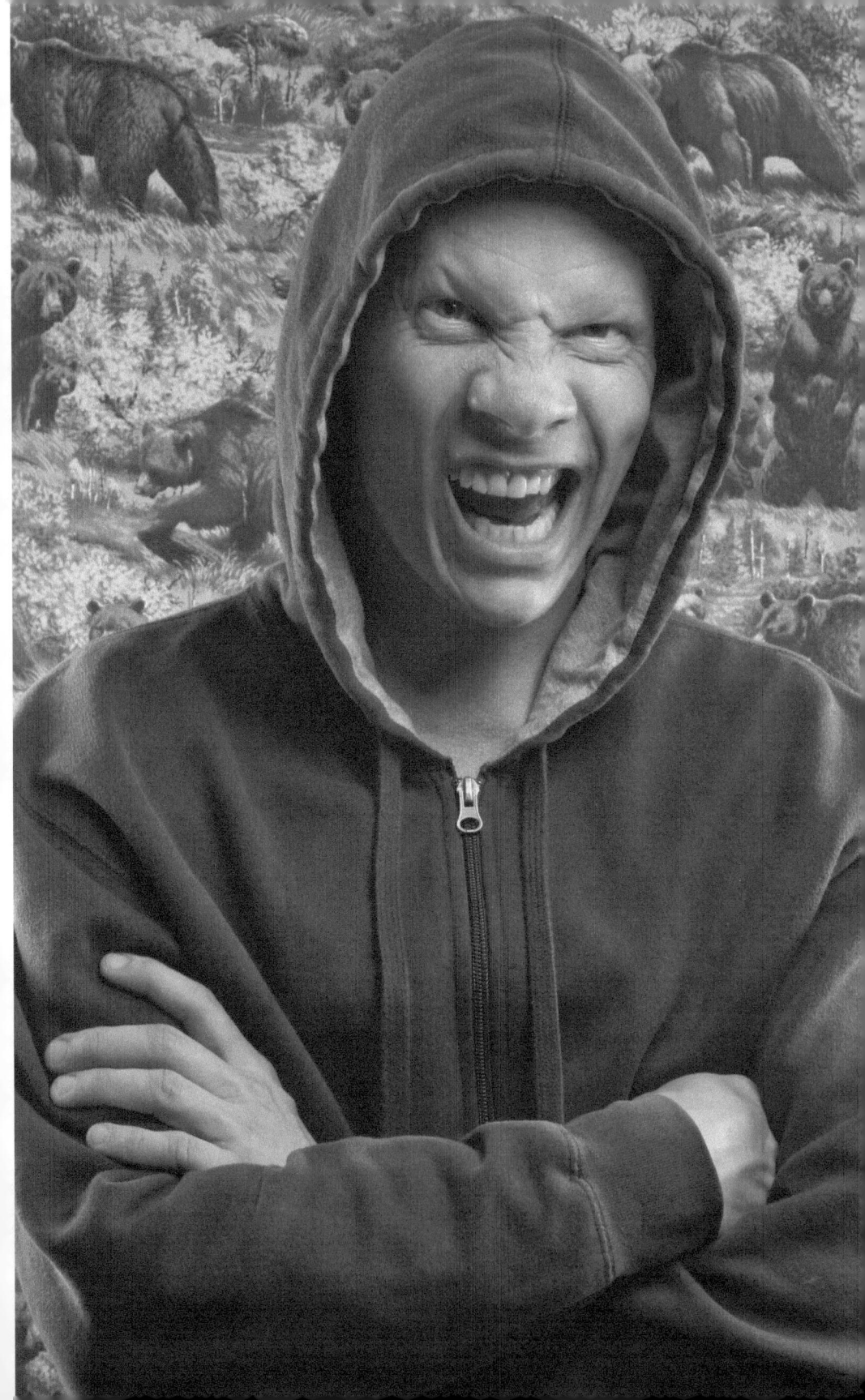

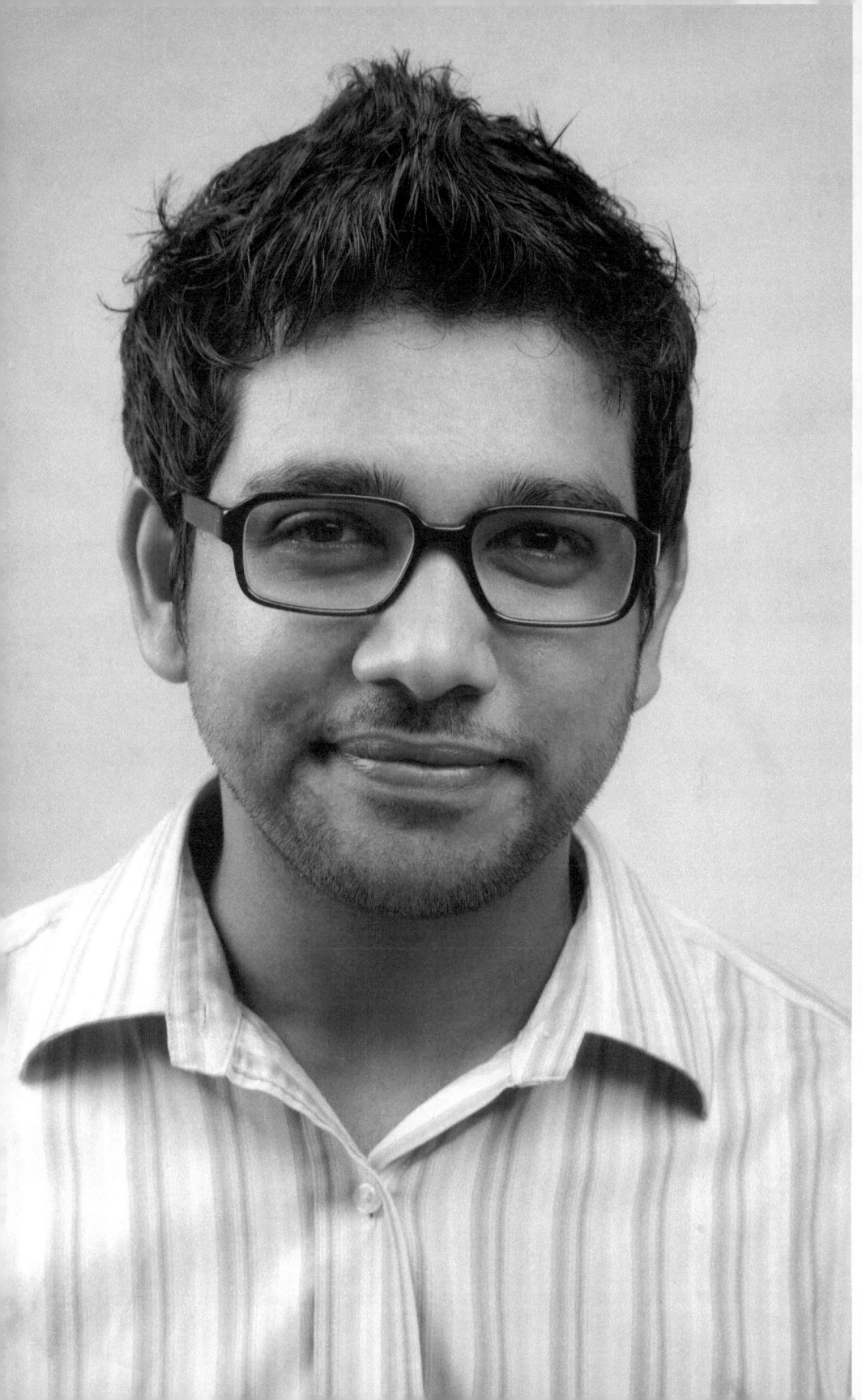

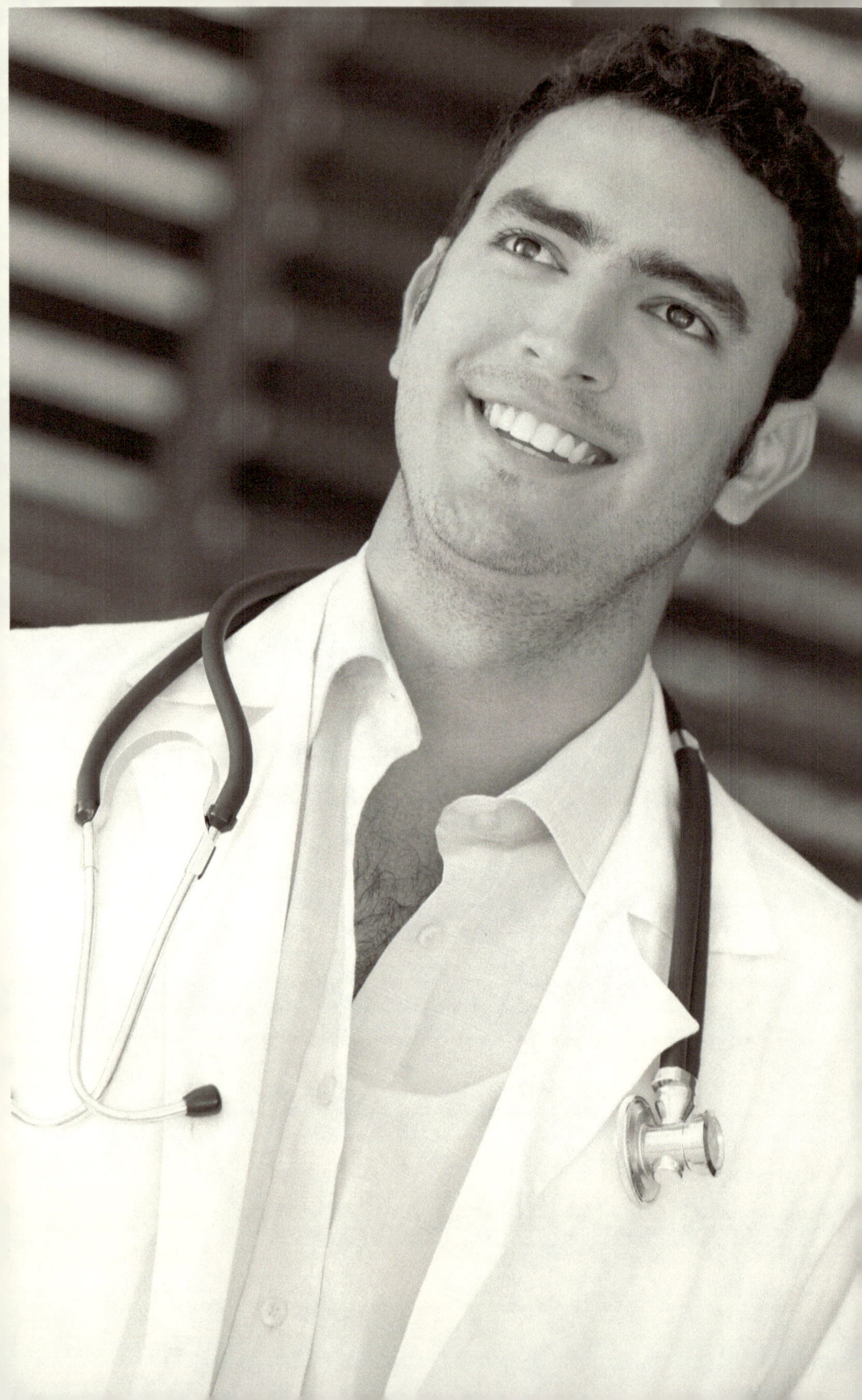

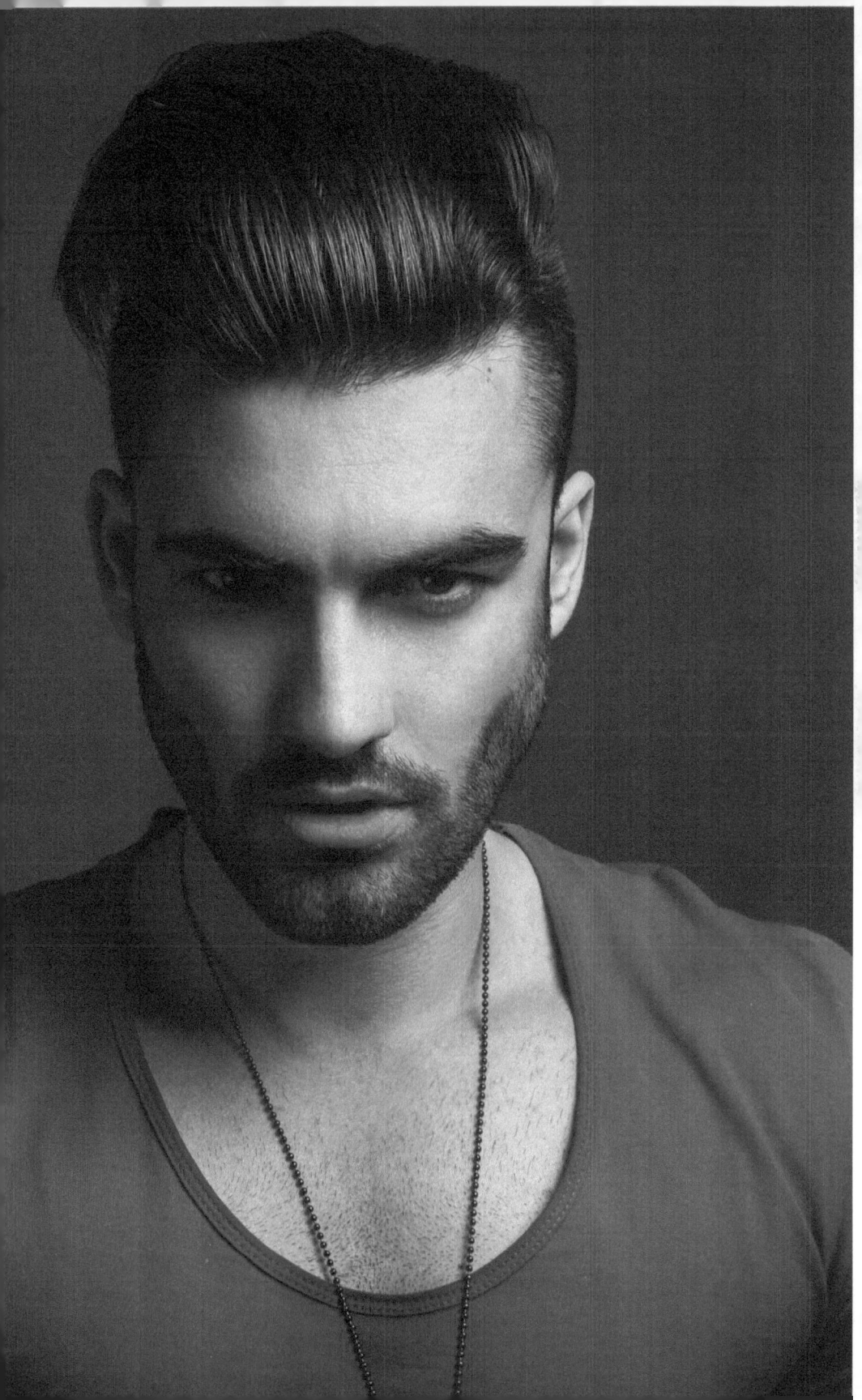

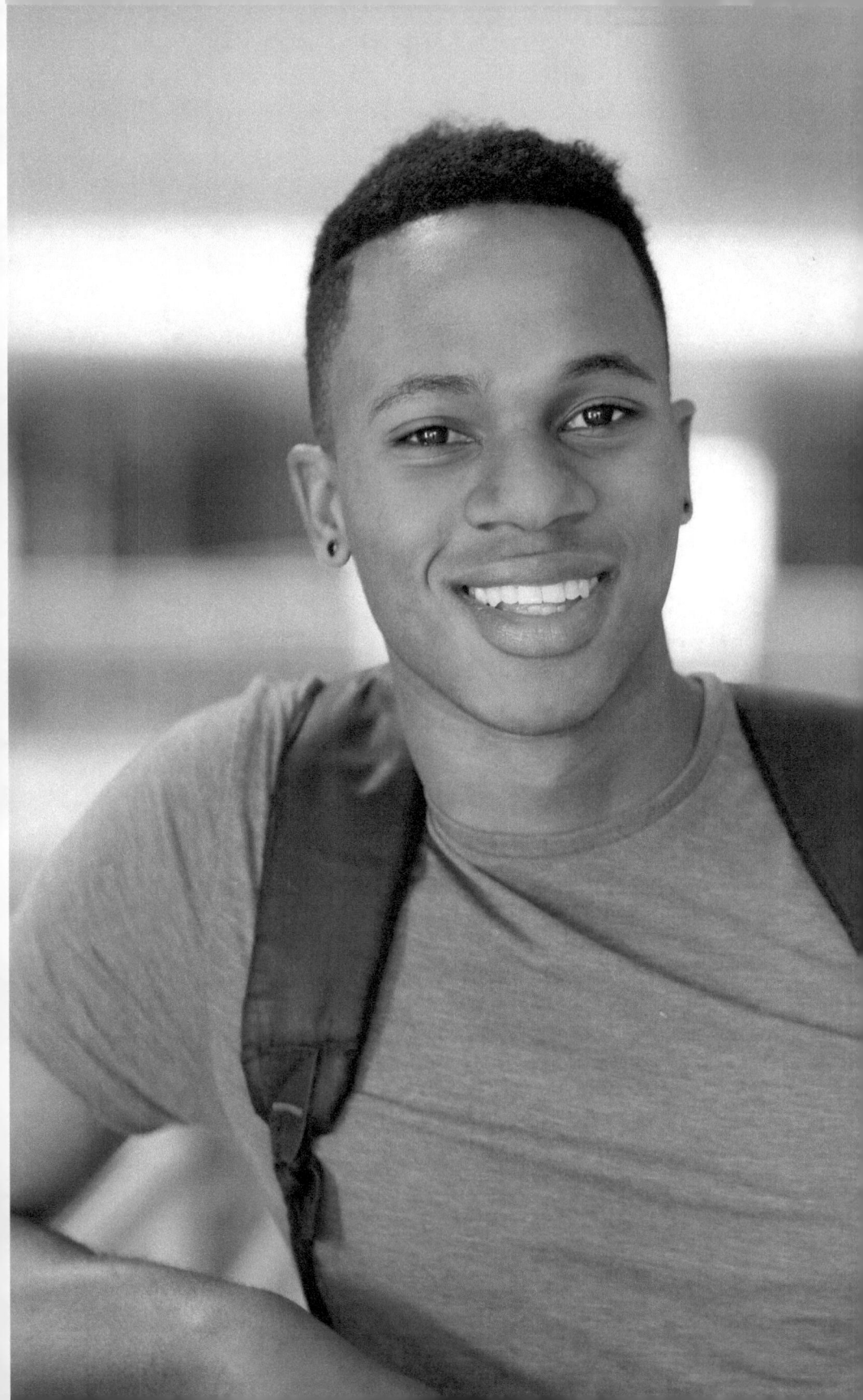

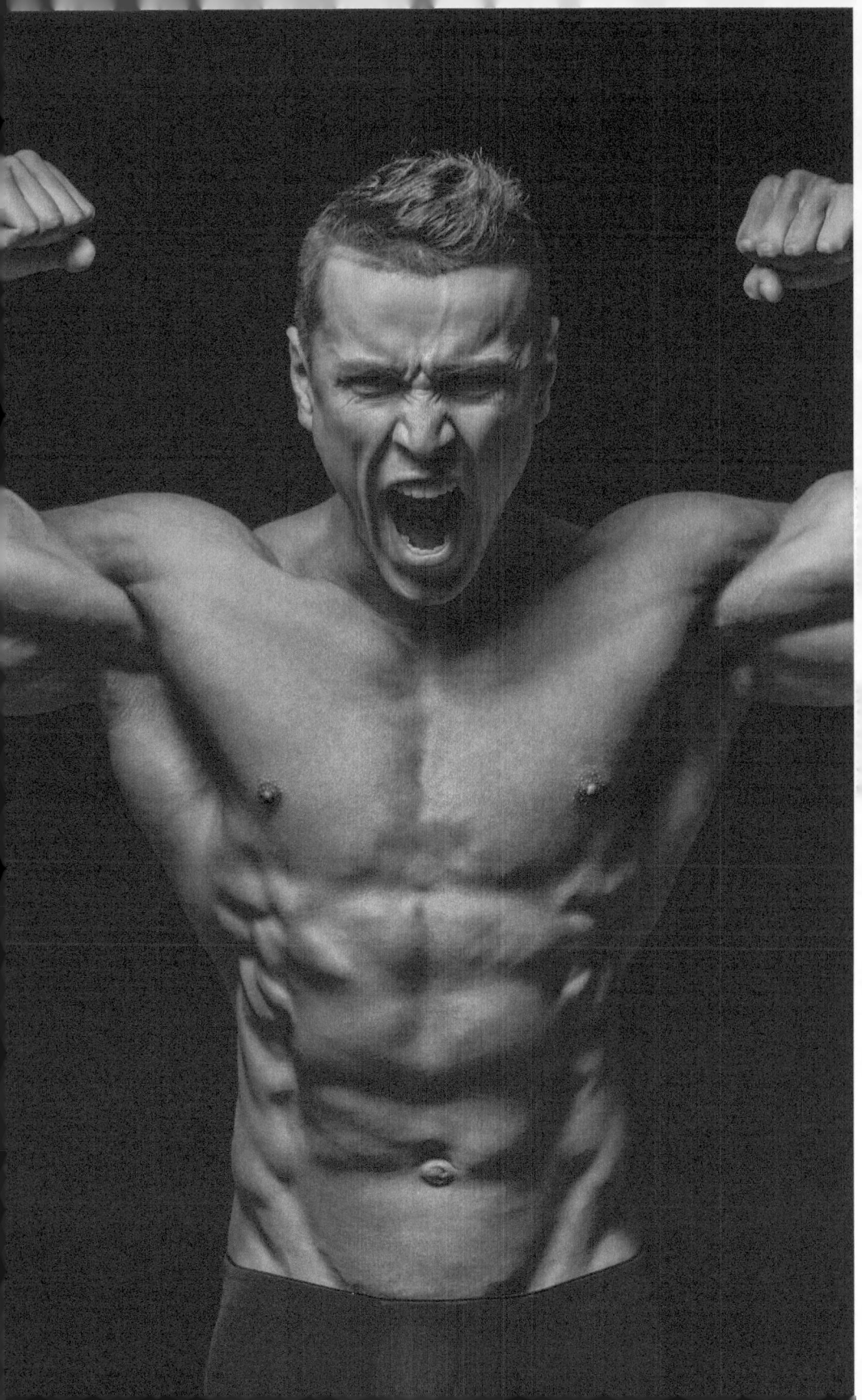

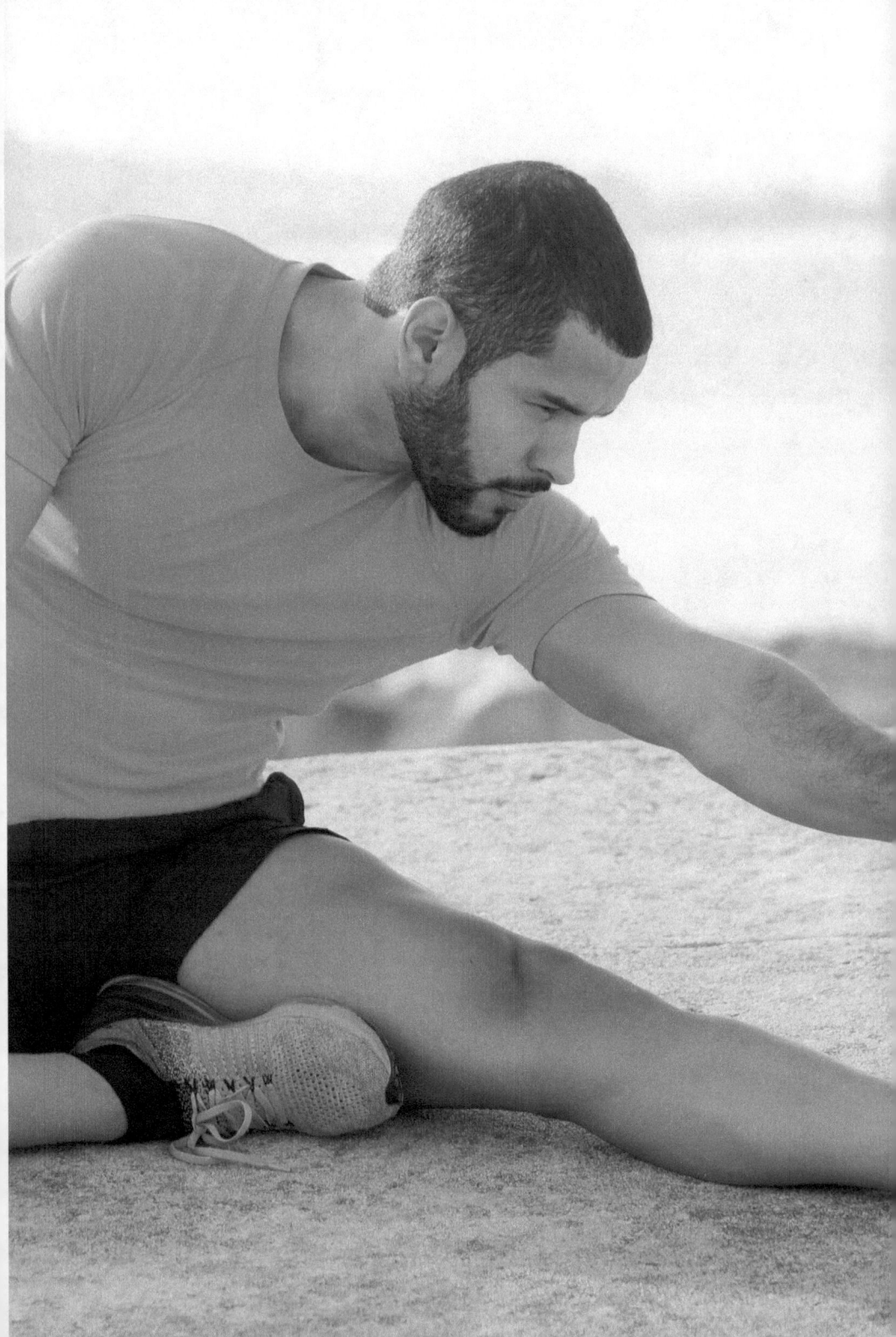

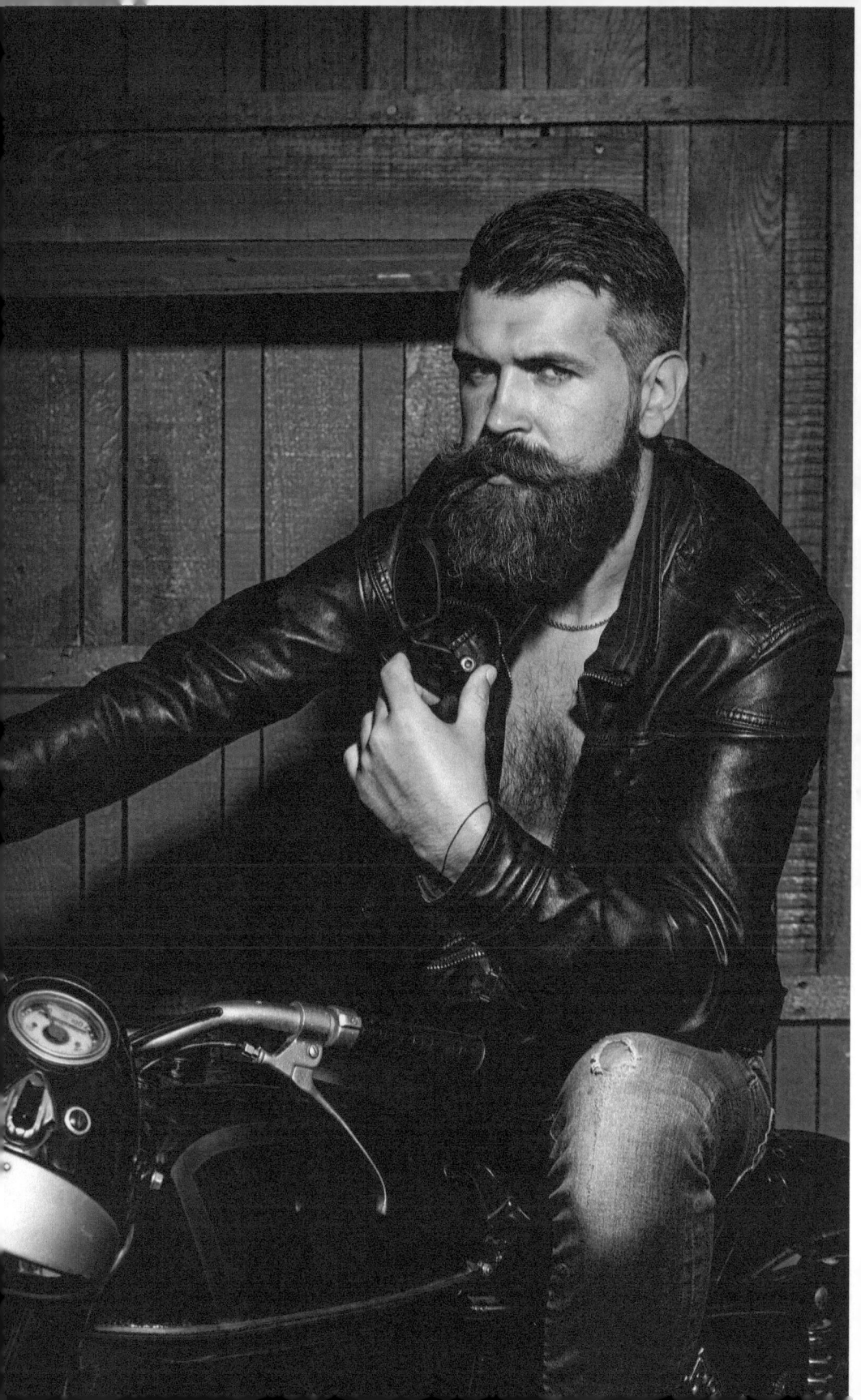

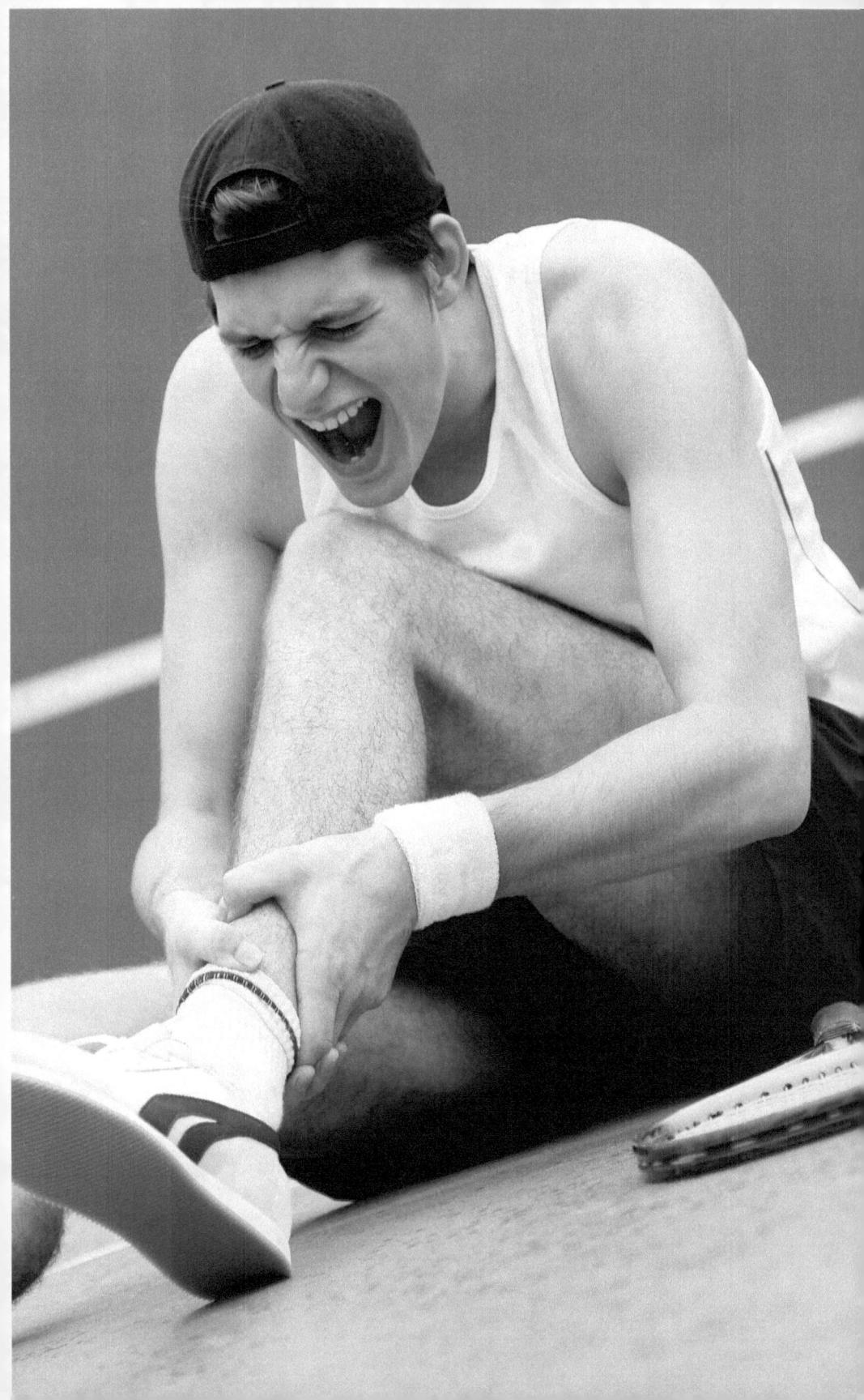

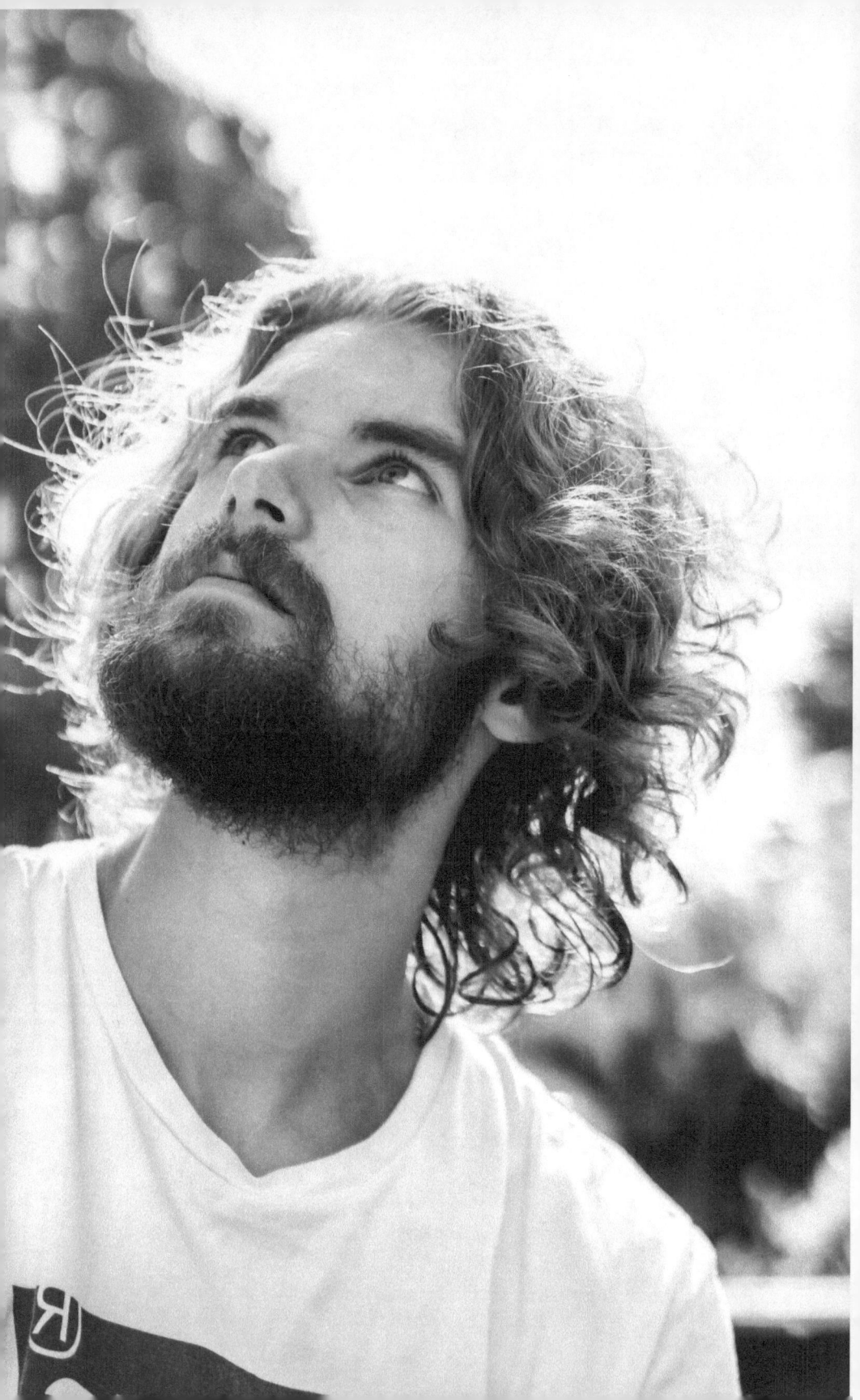

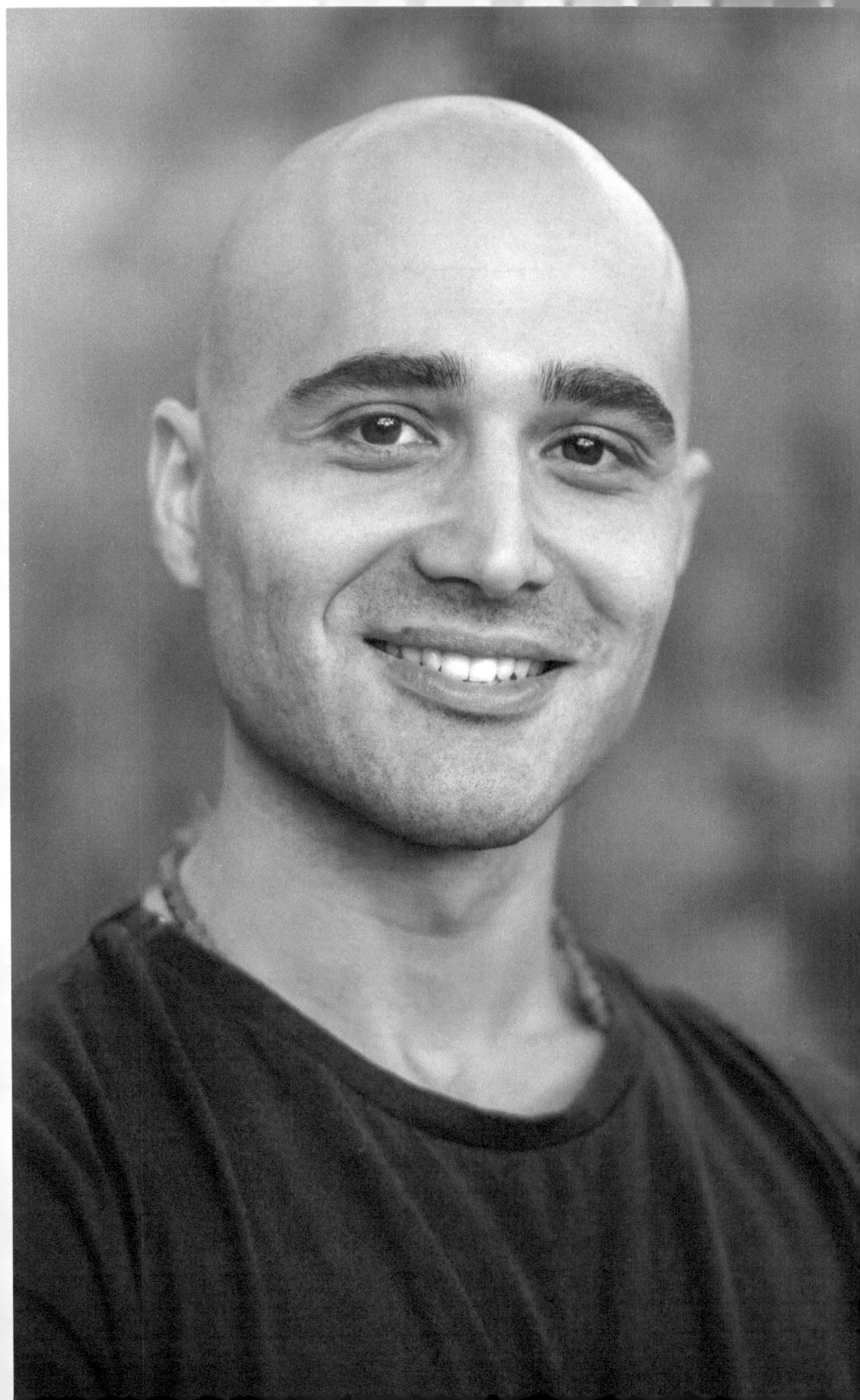

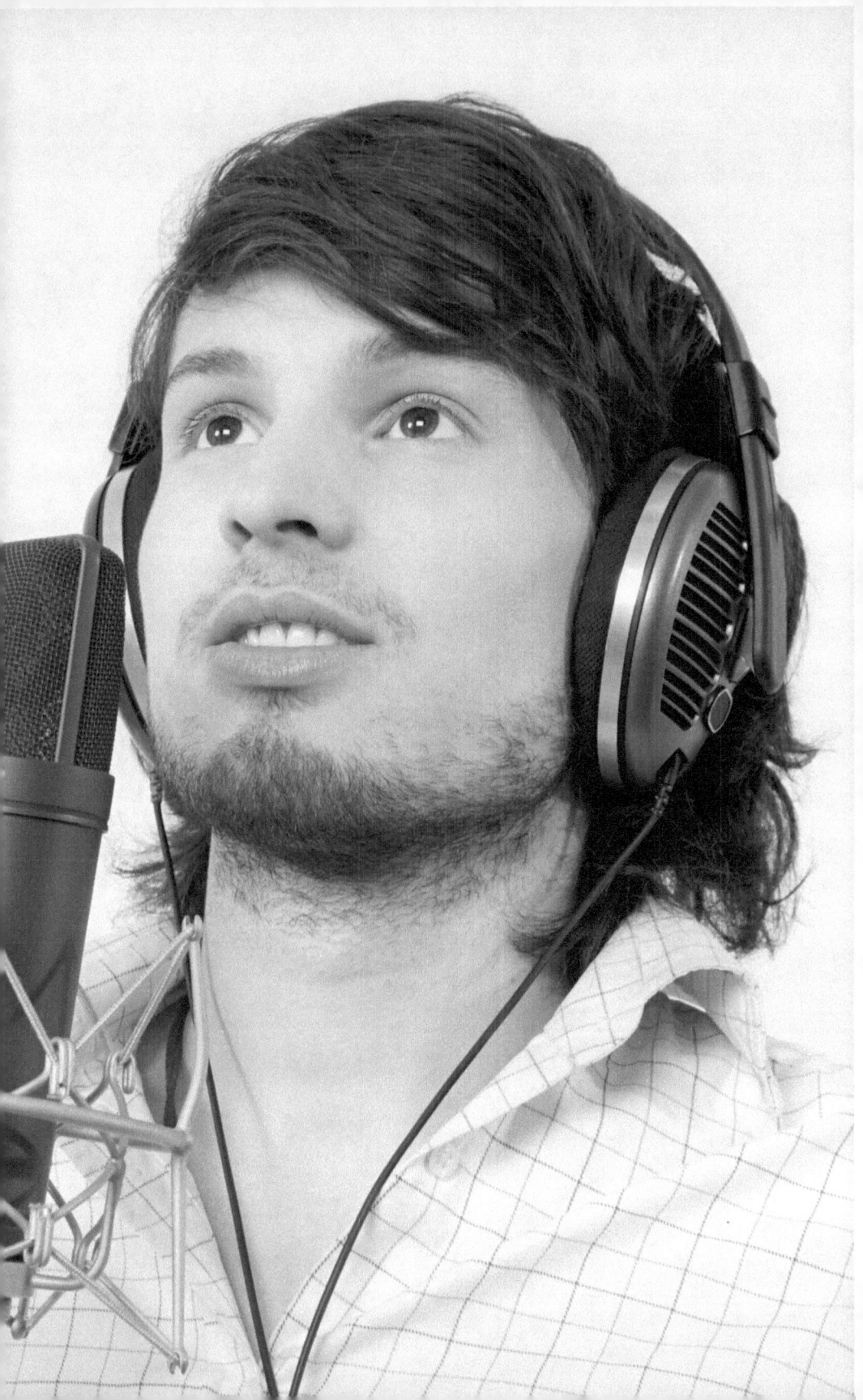

"The face is the mirror of the mind"

St. Jerome

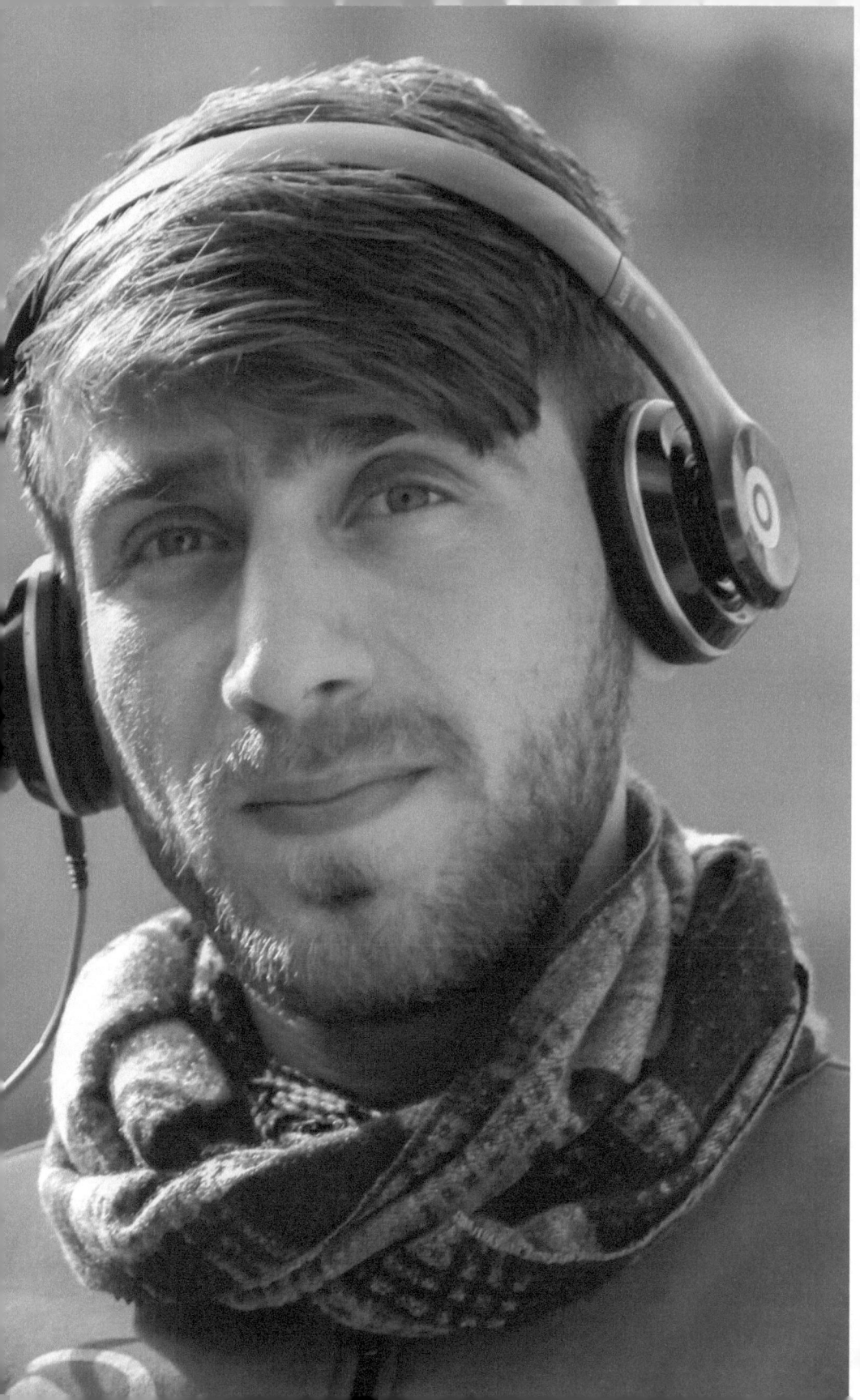

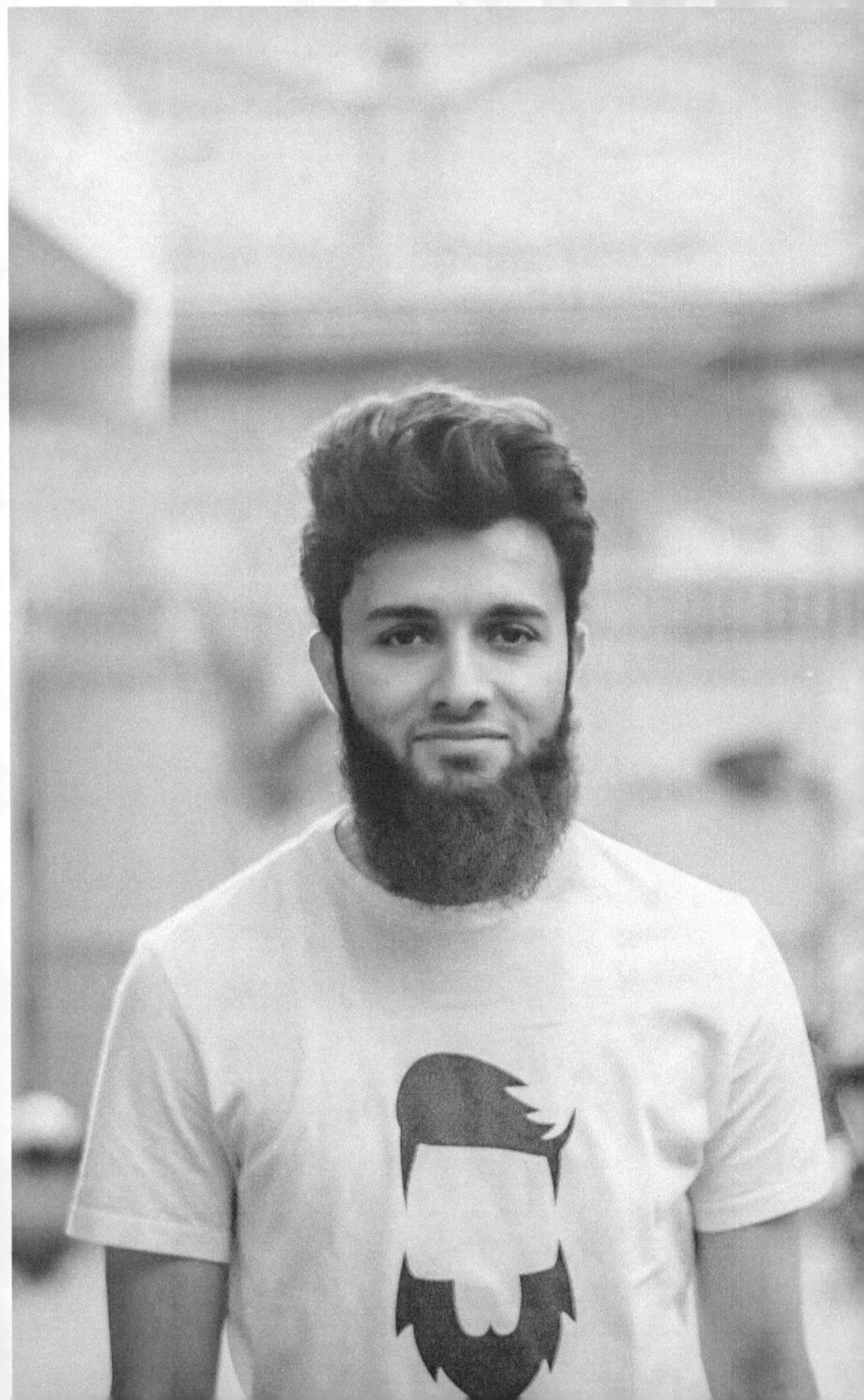

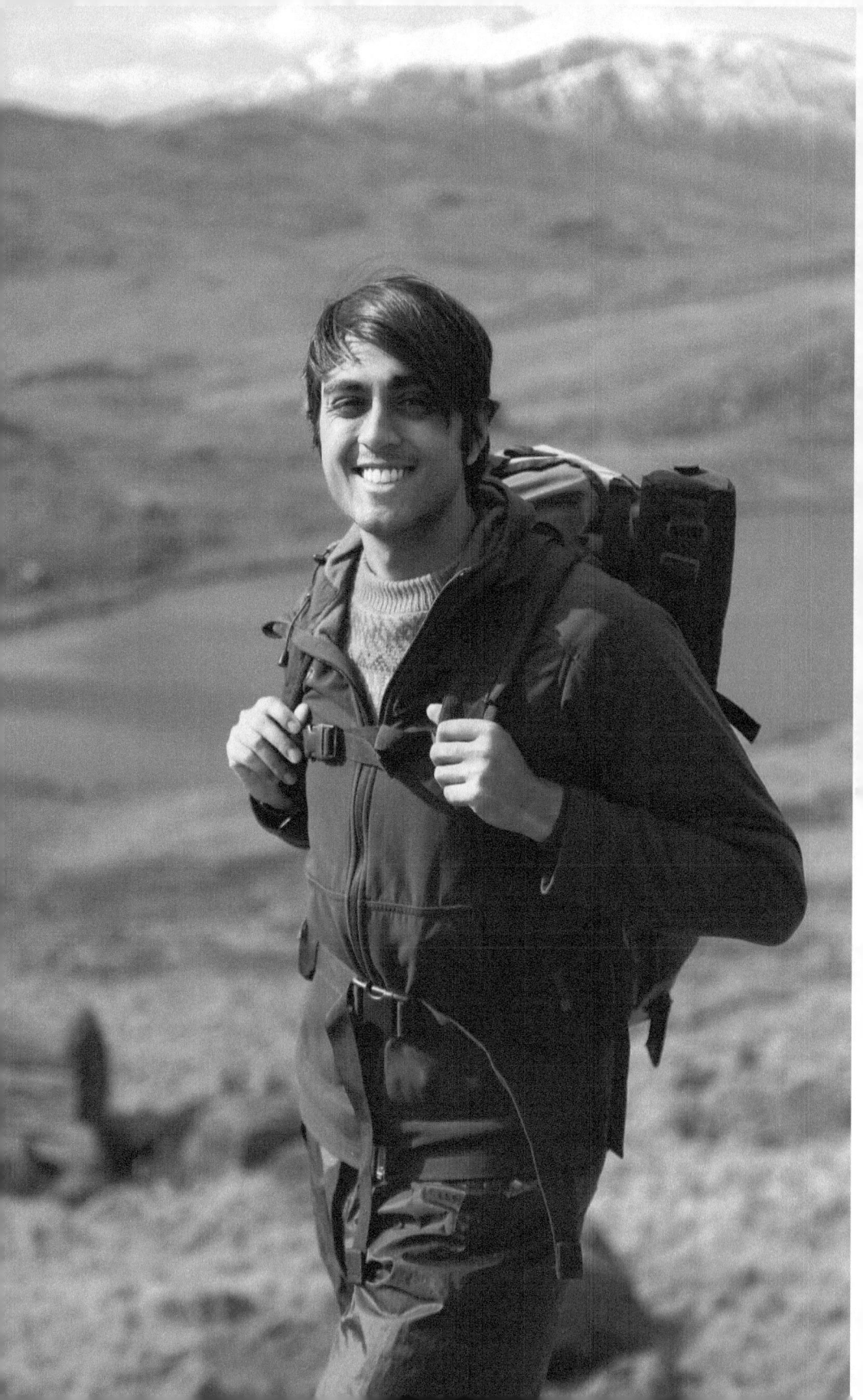

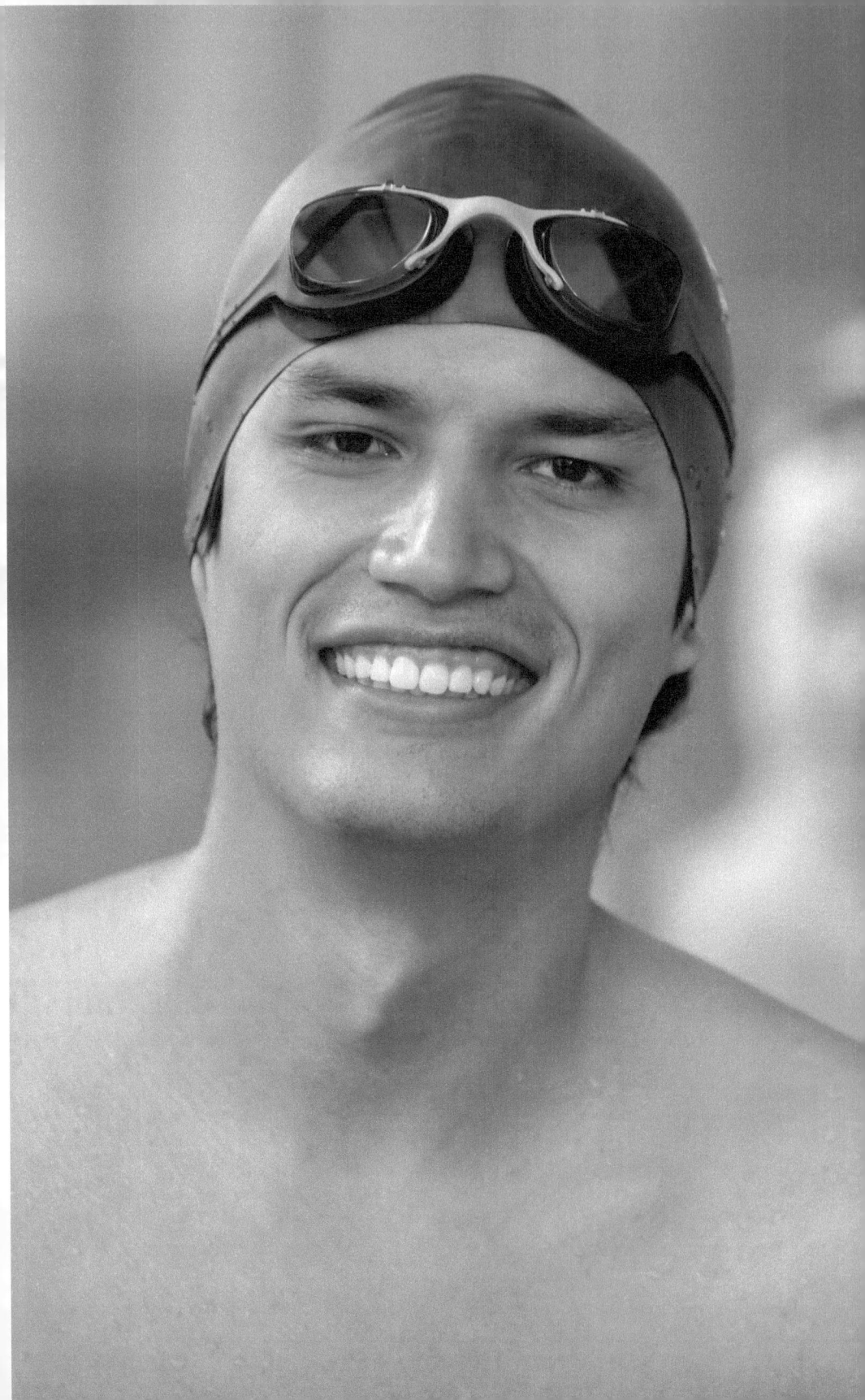

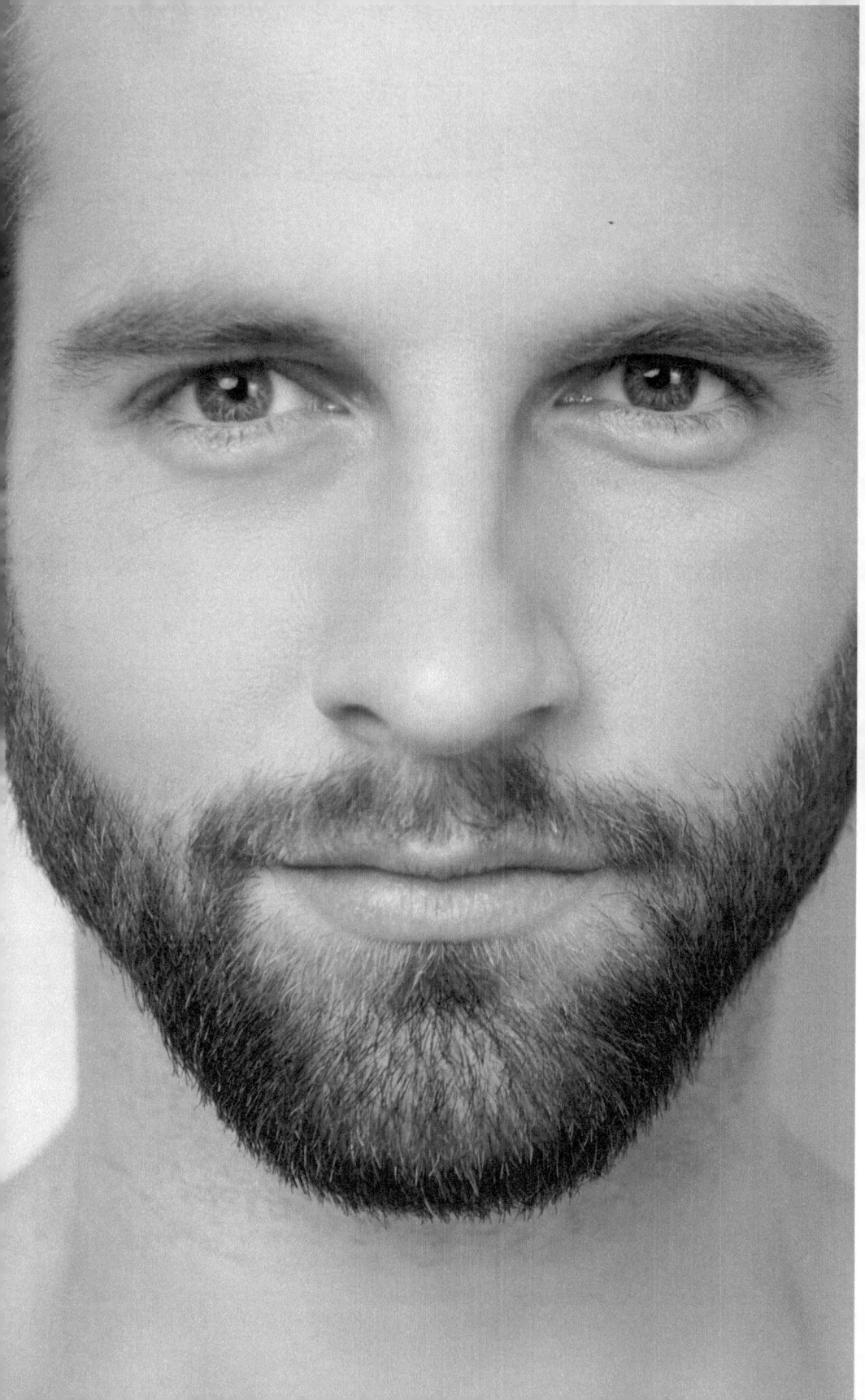

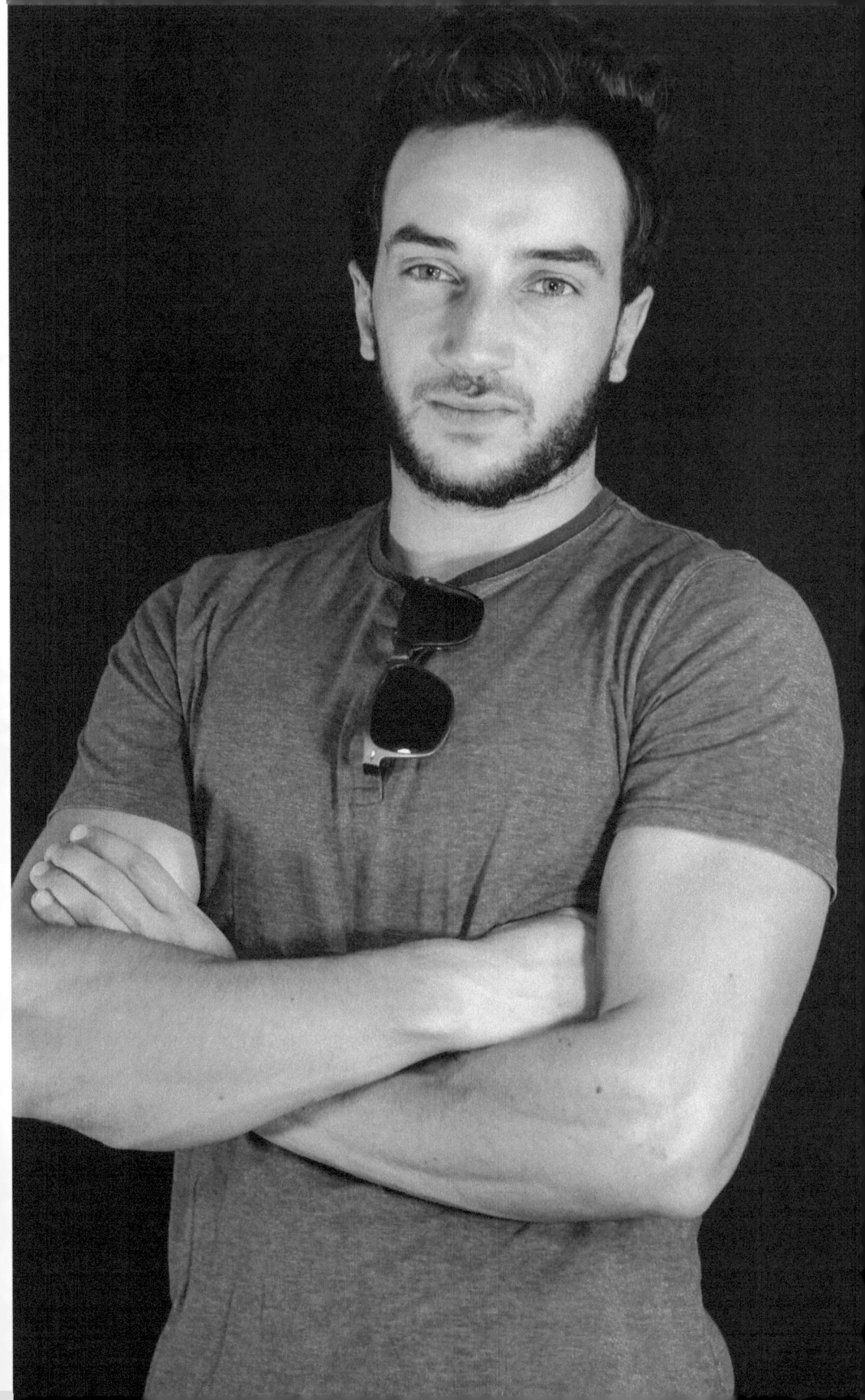

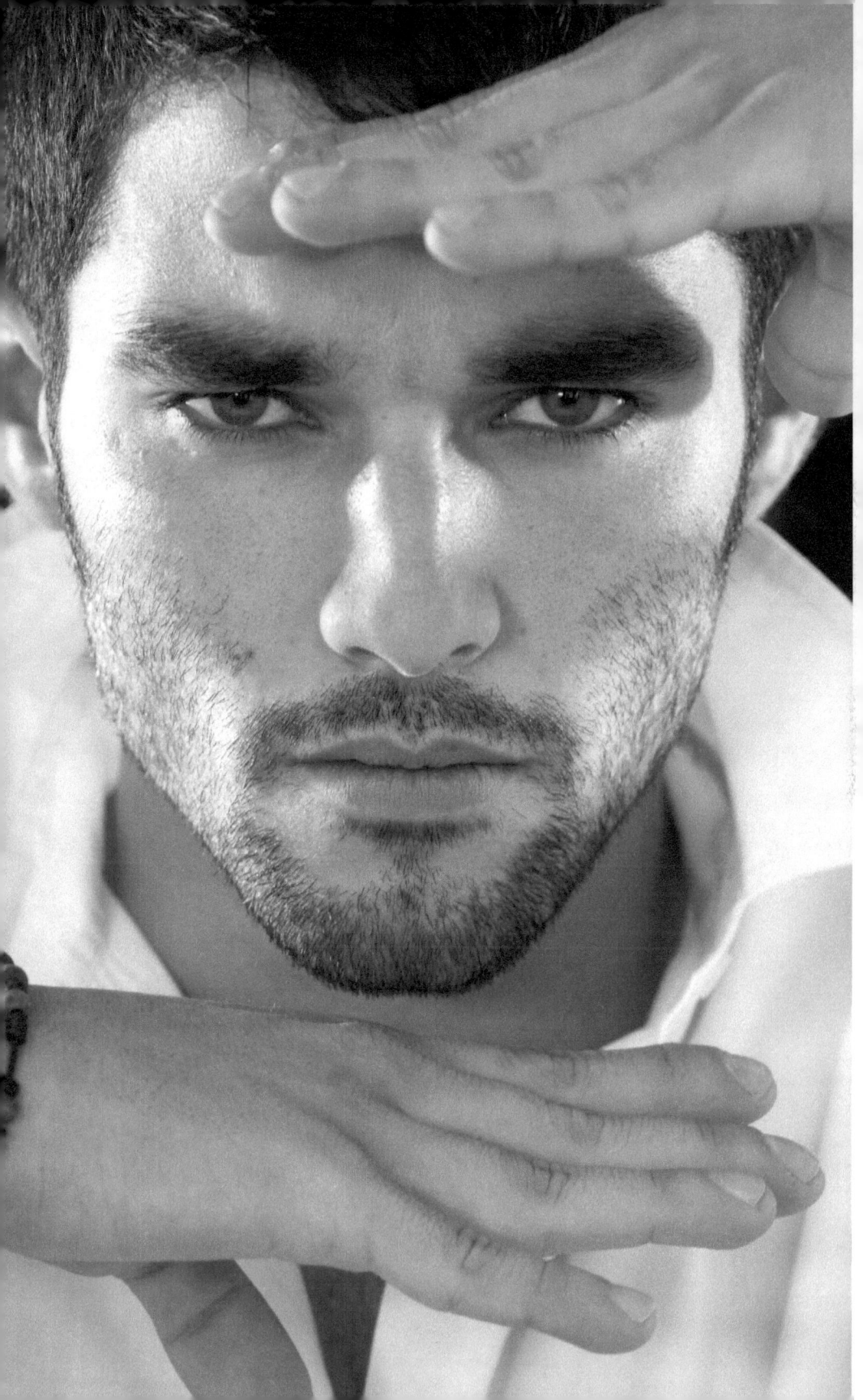

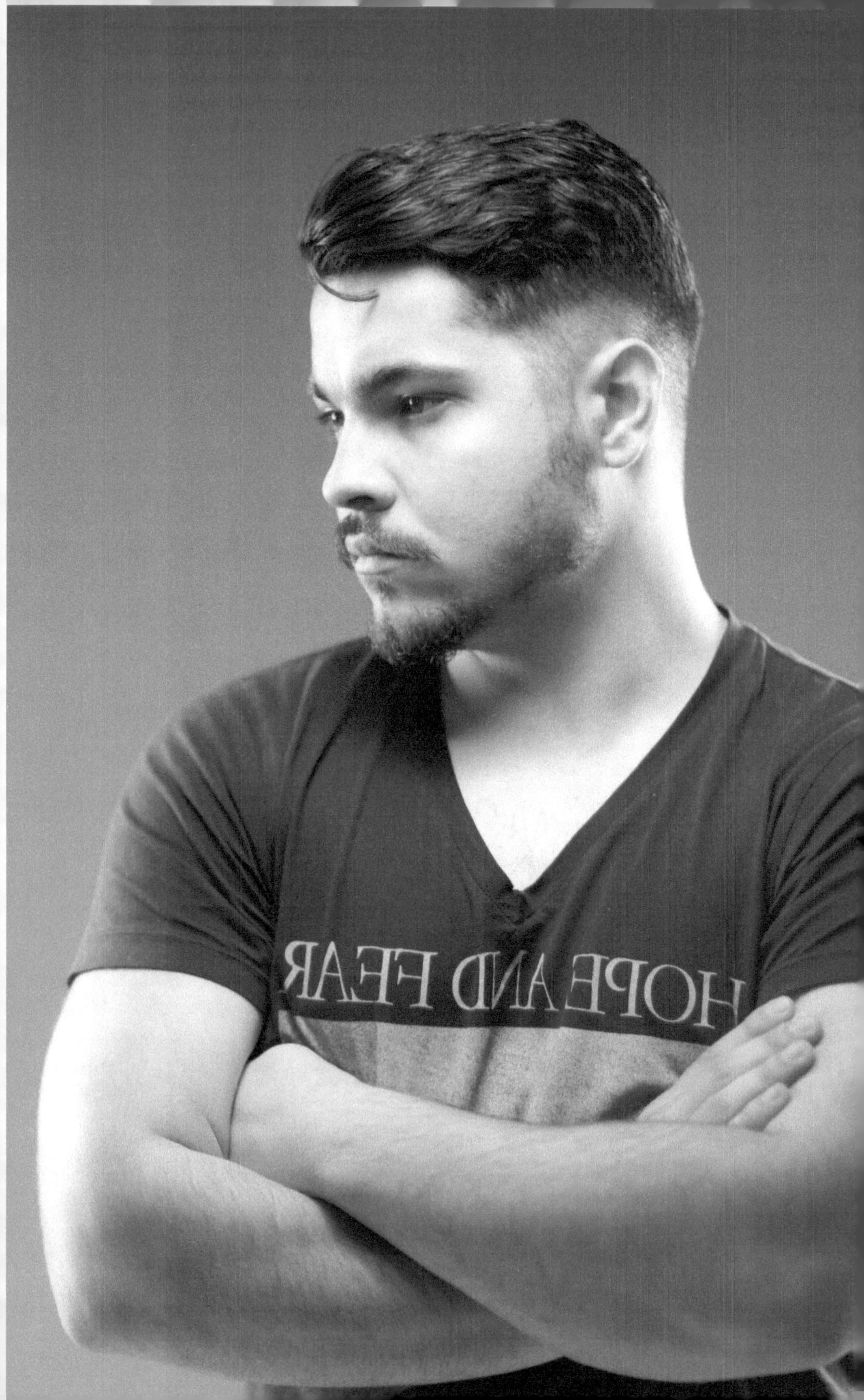
HOPE AND FEAR

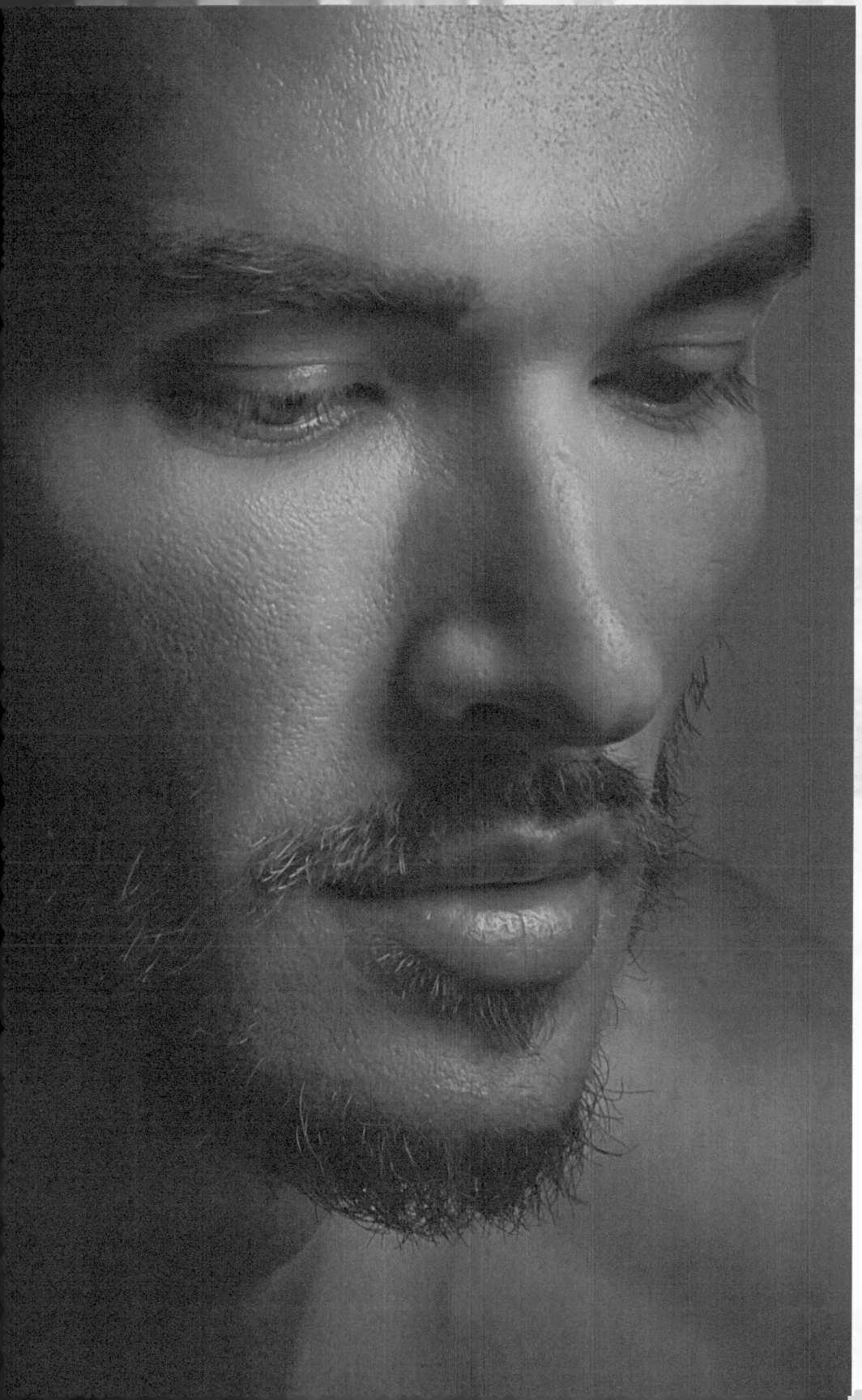

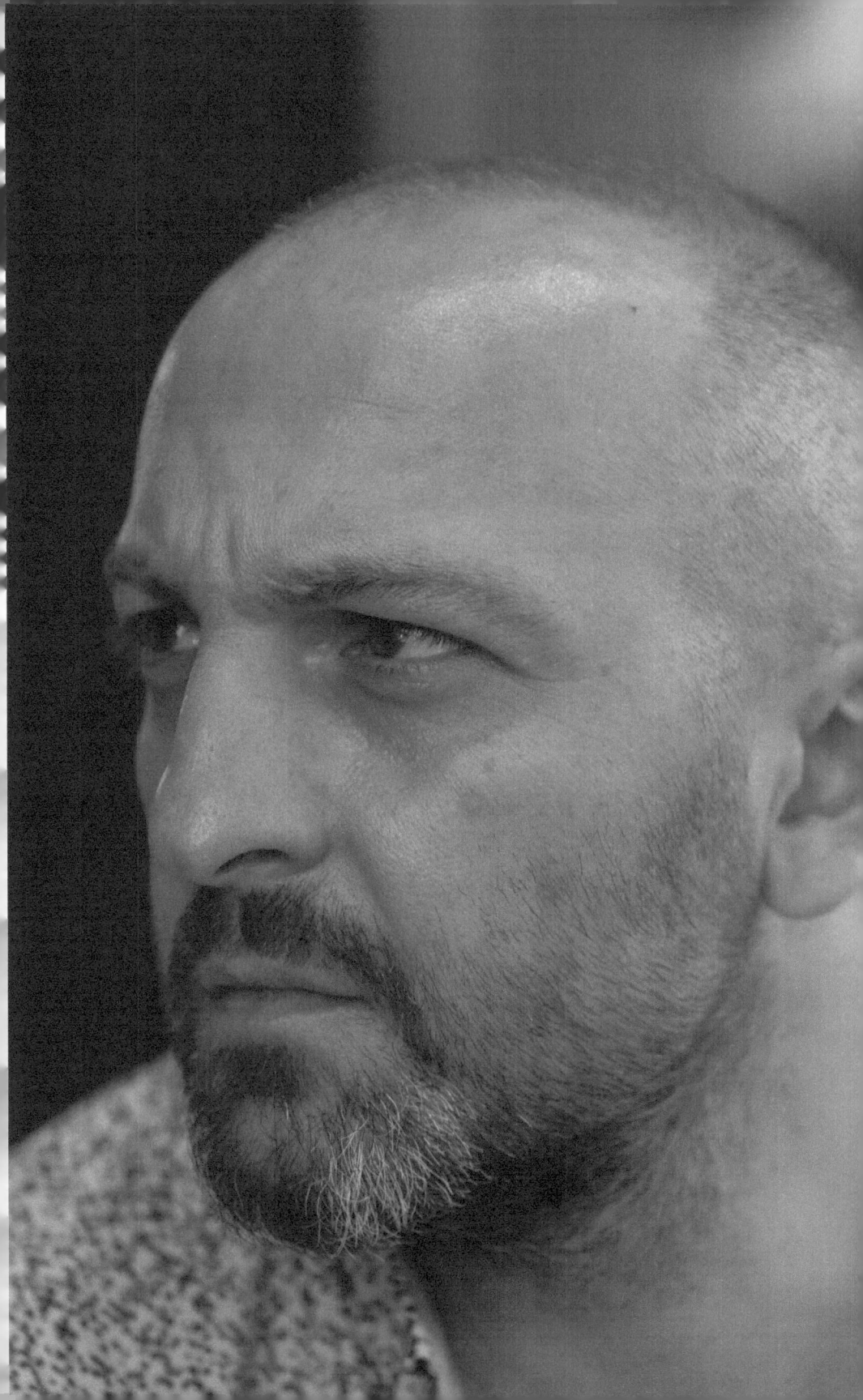

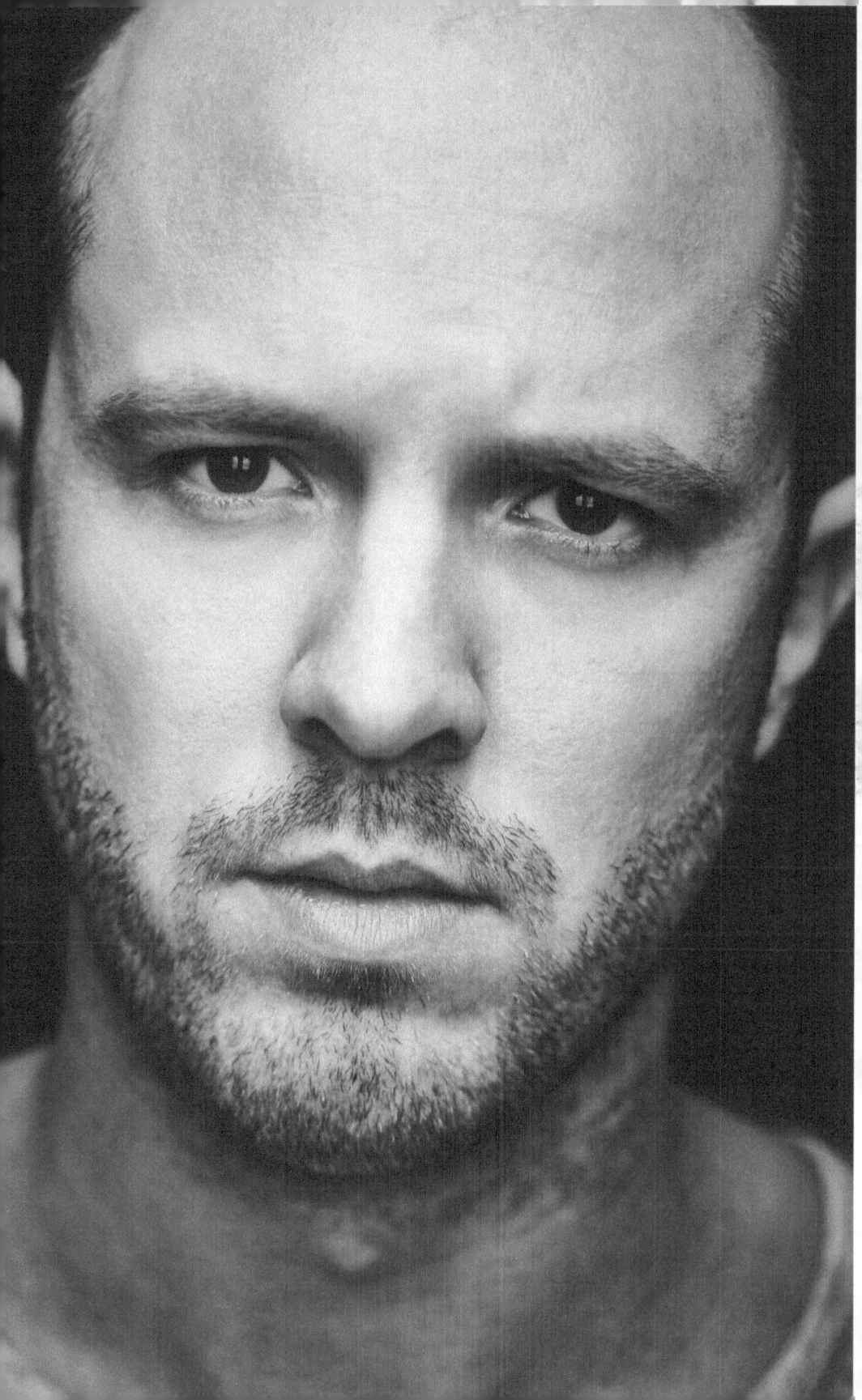

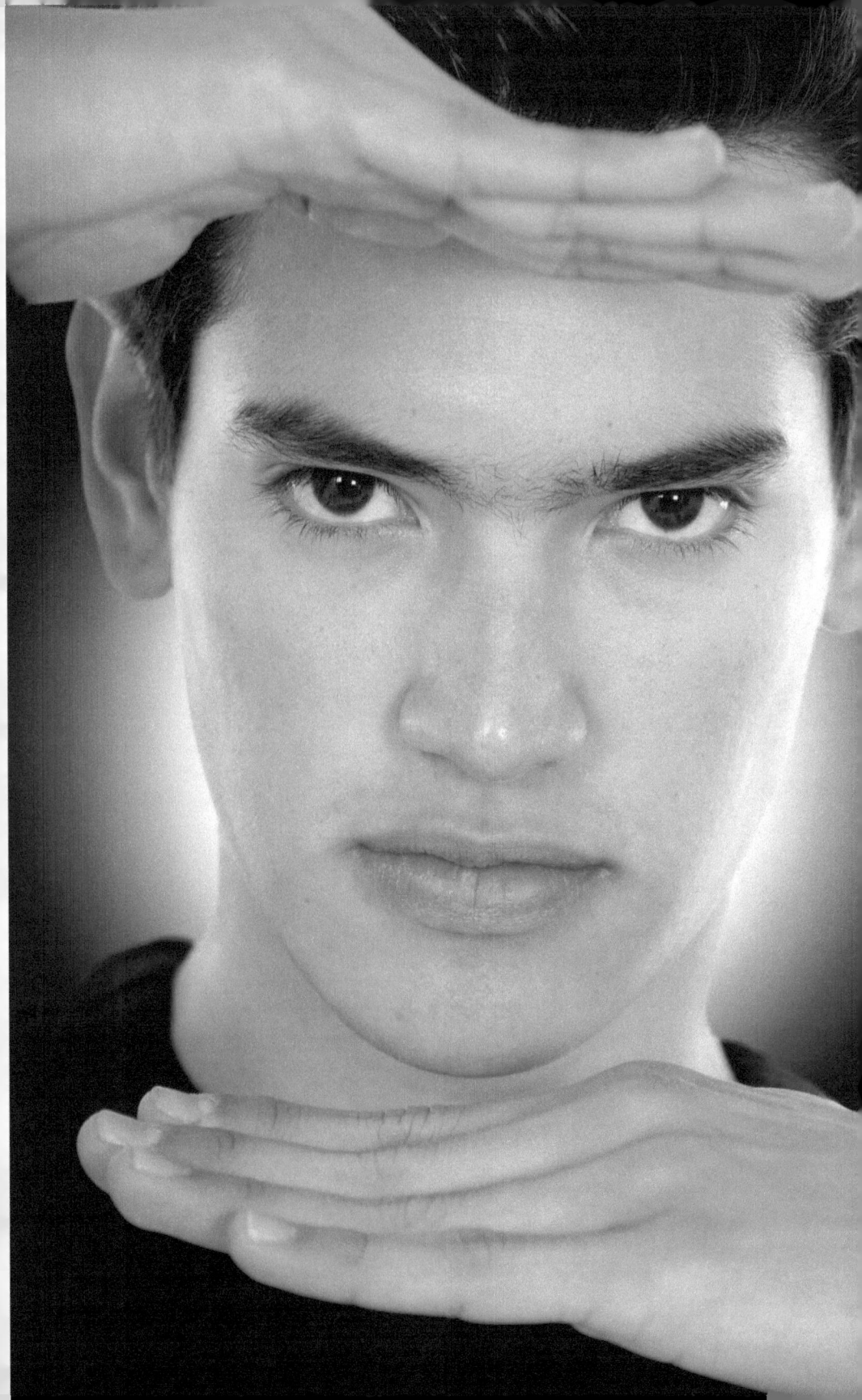

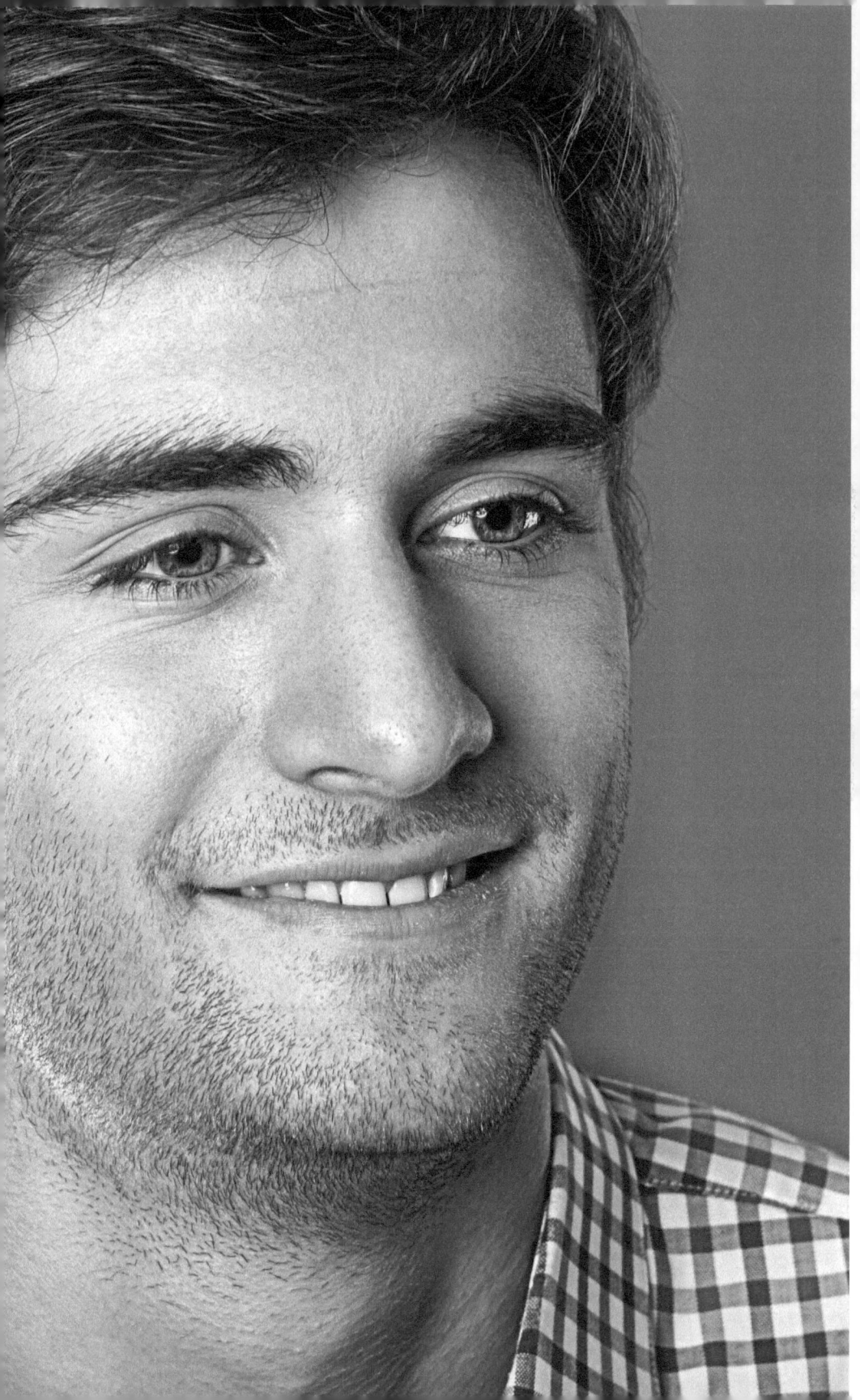

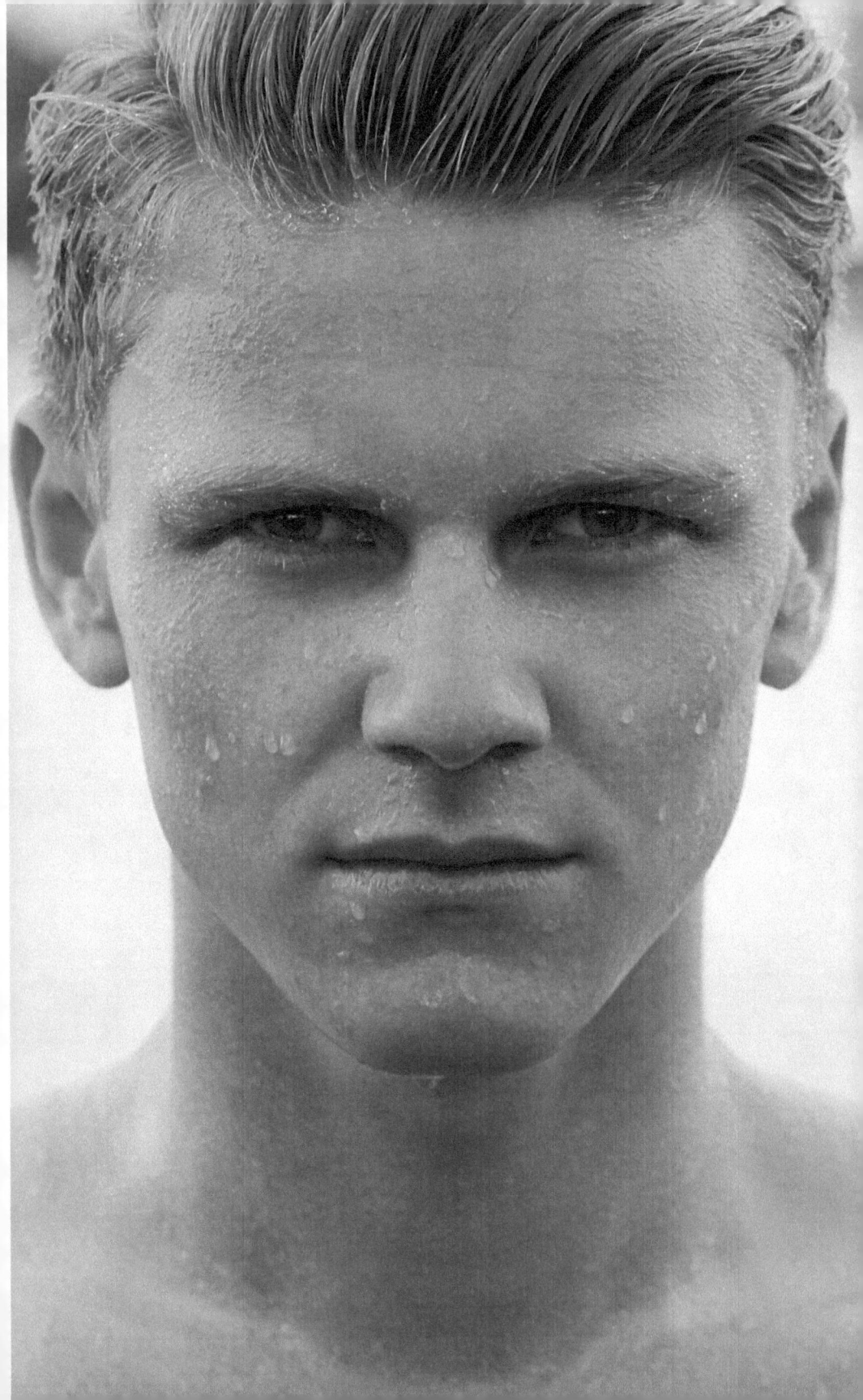

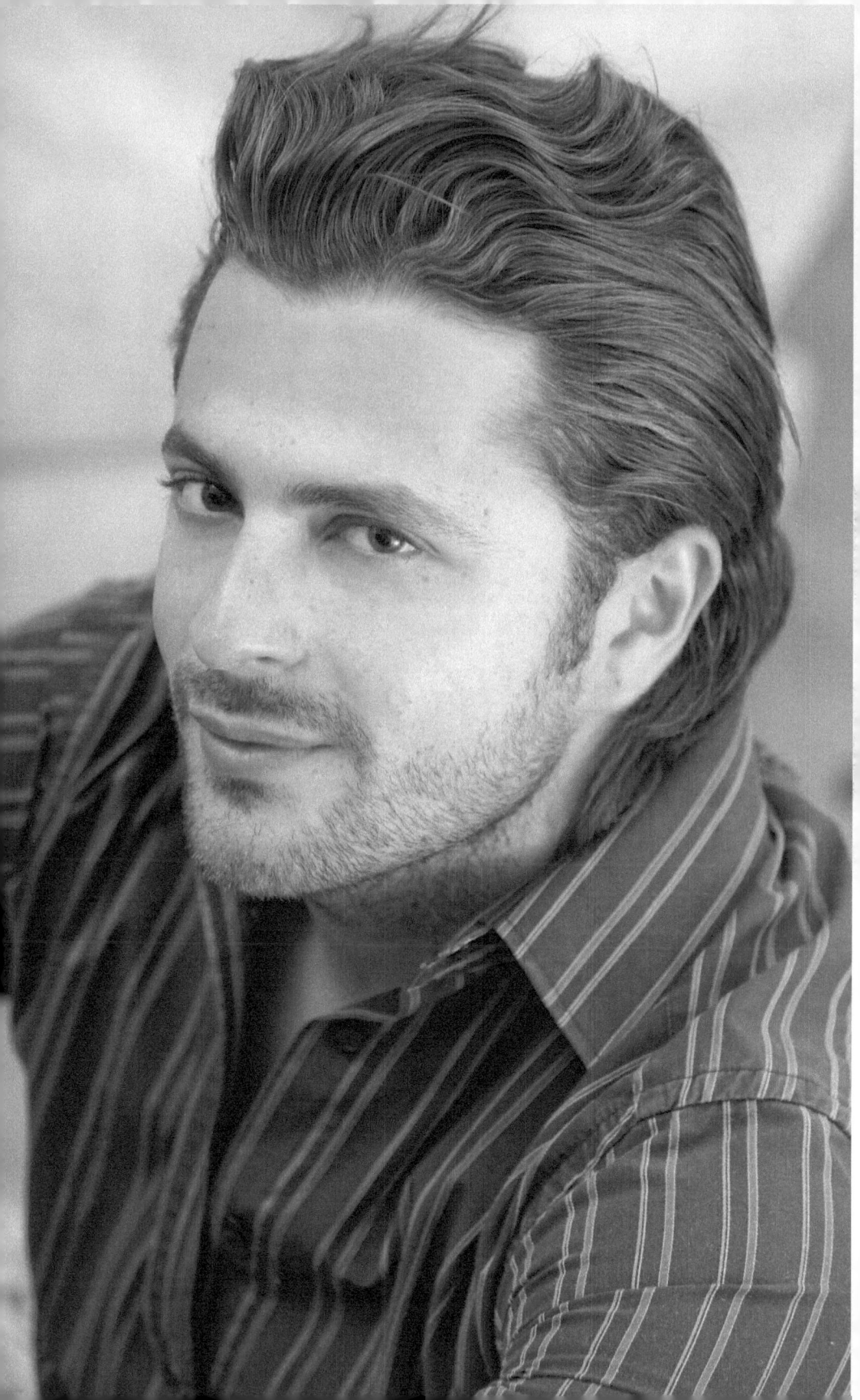

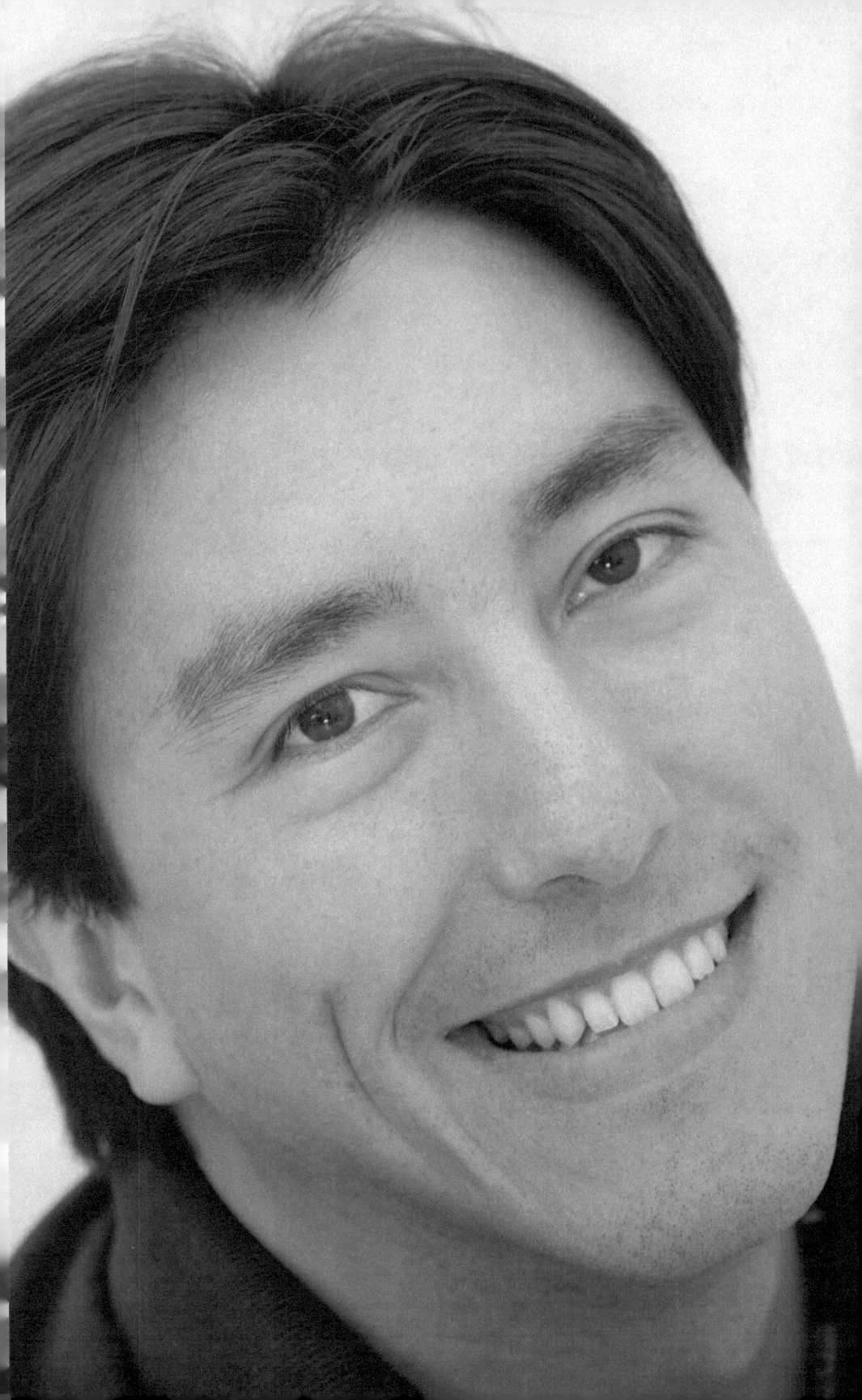

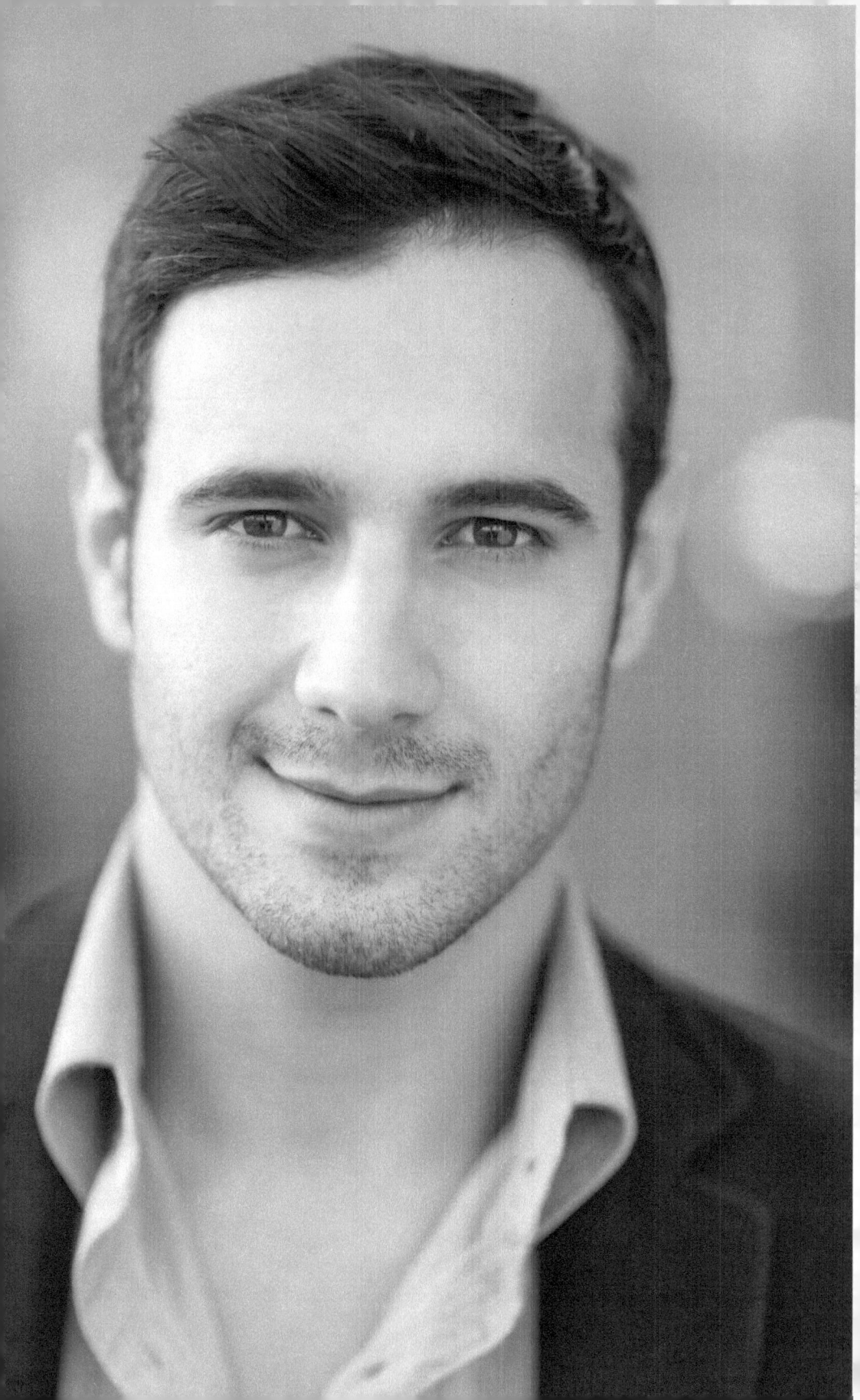

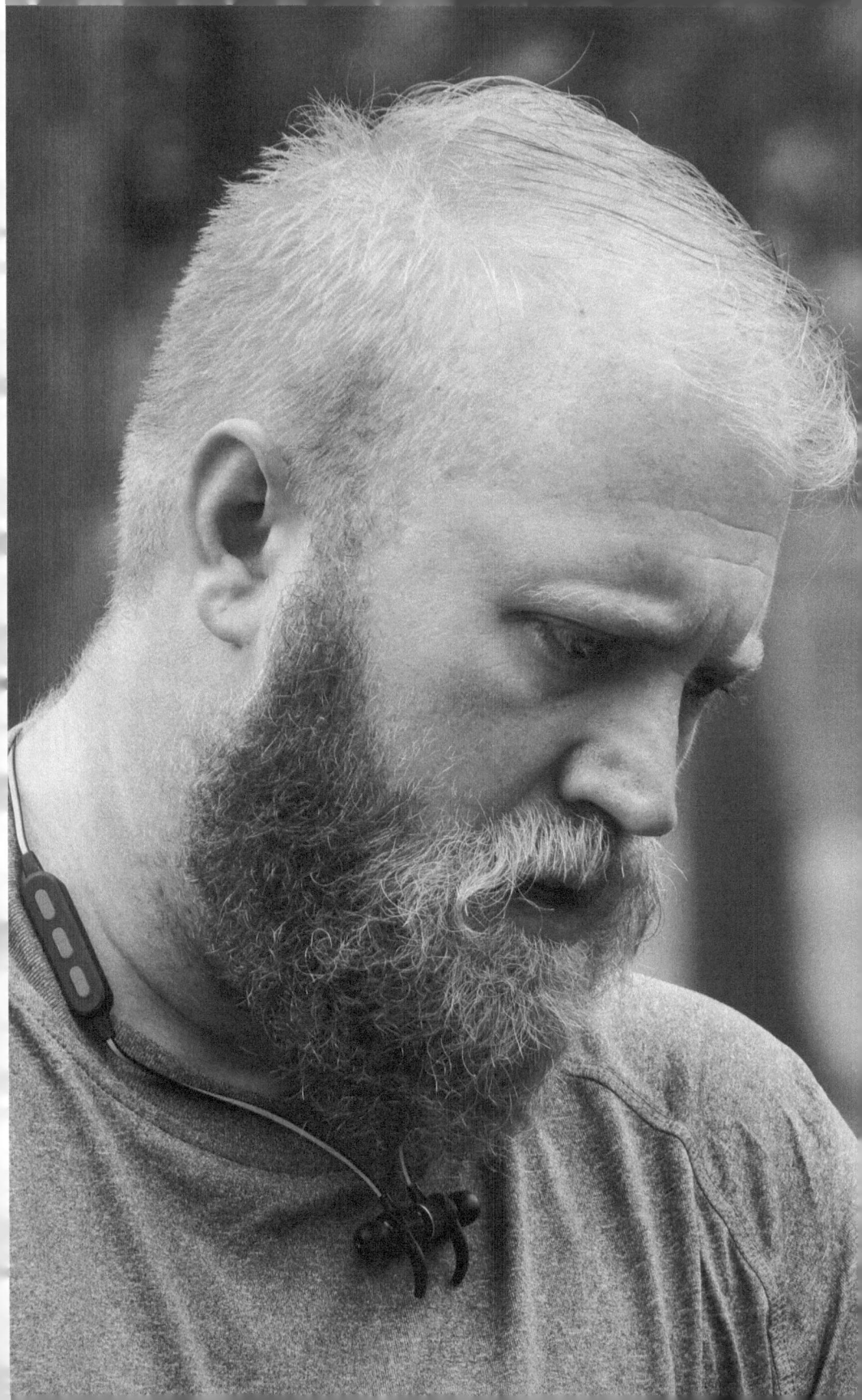

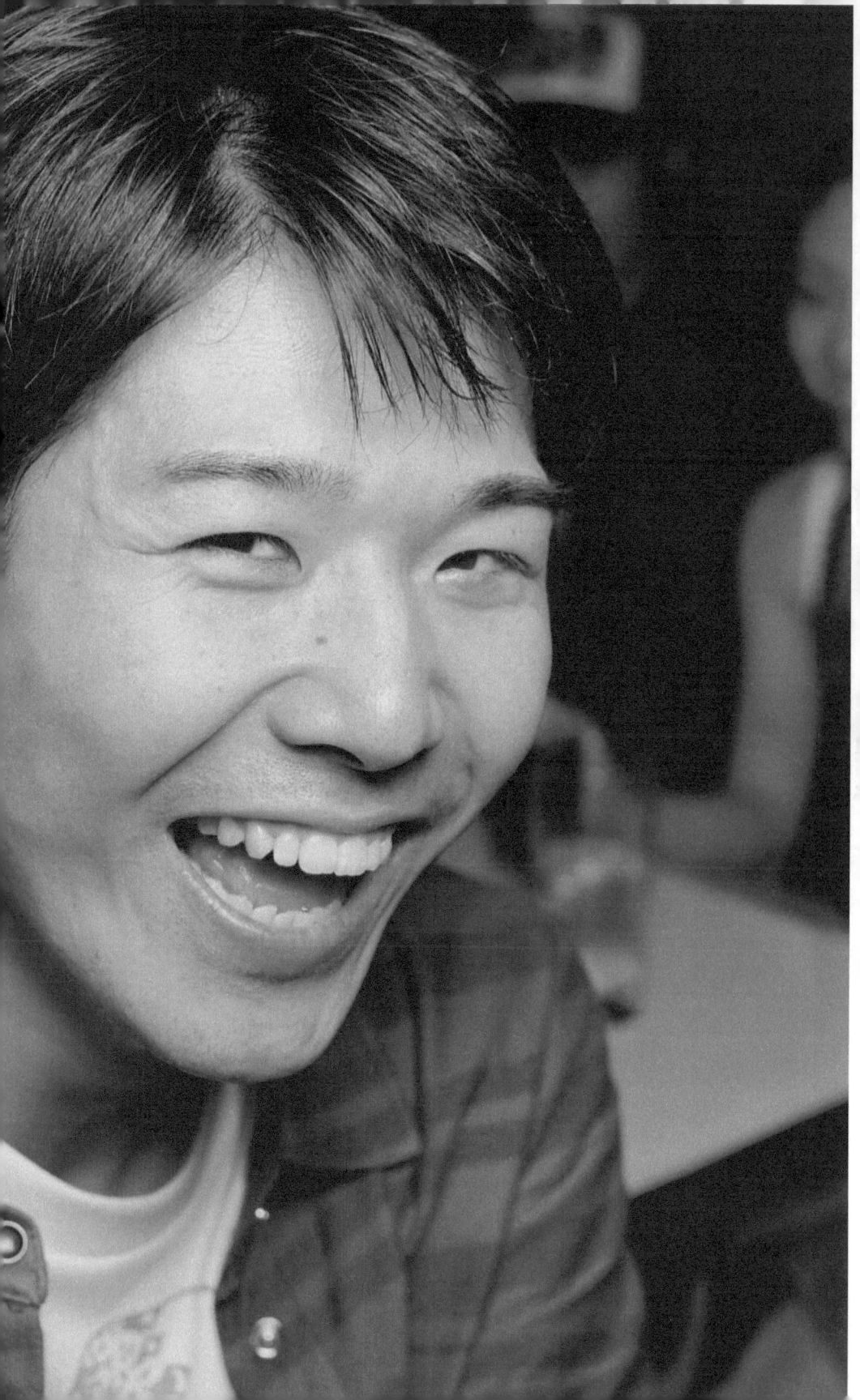

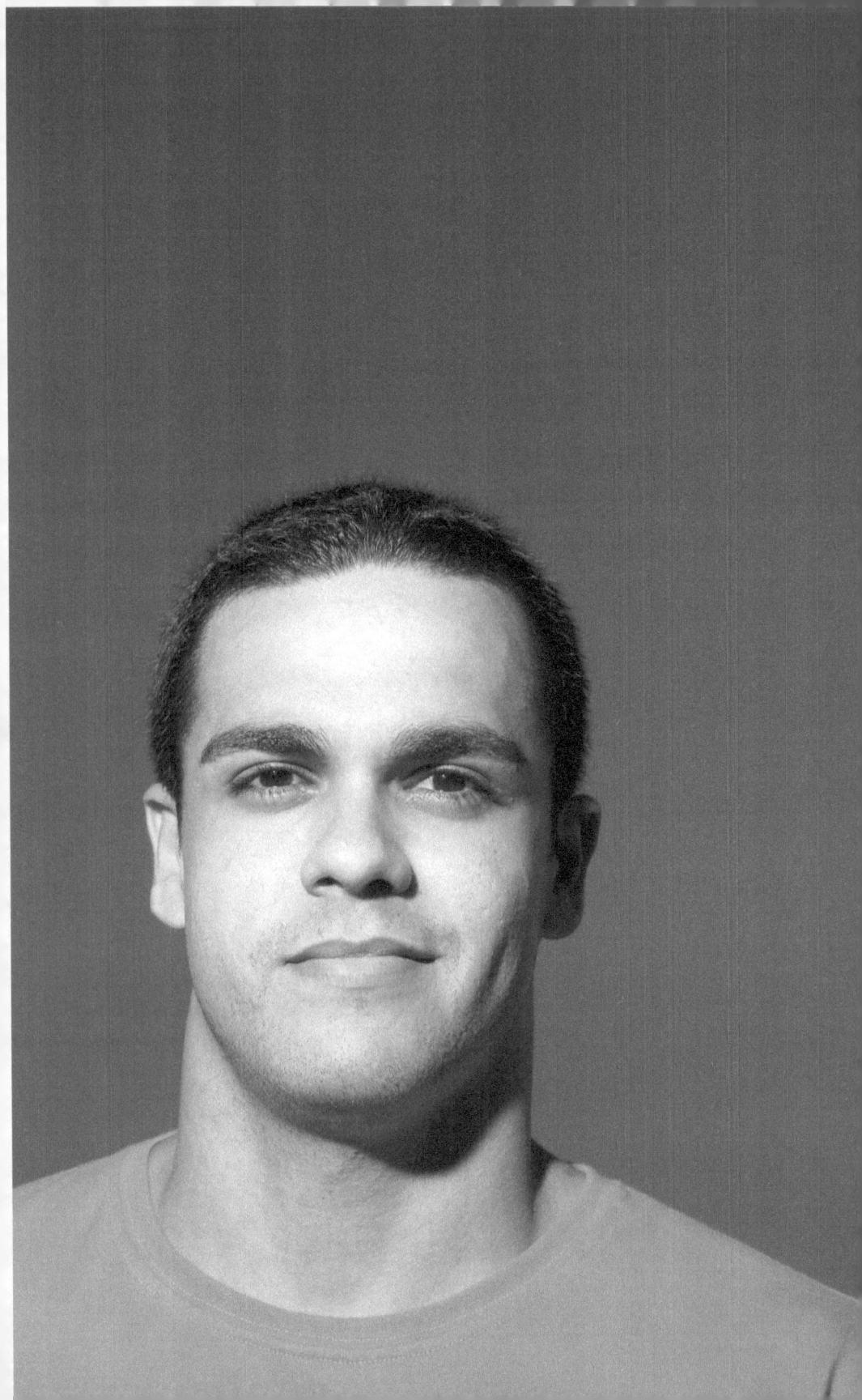

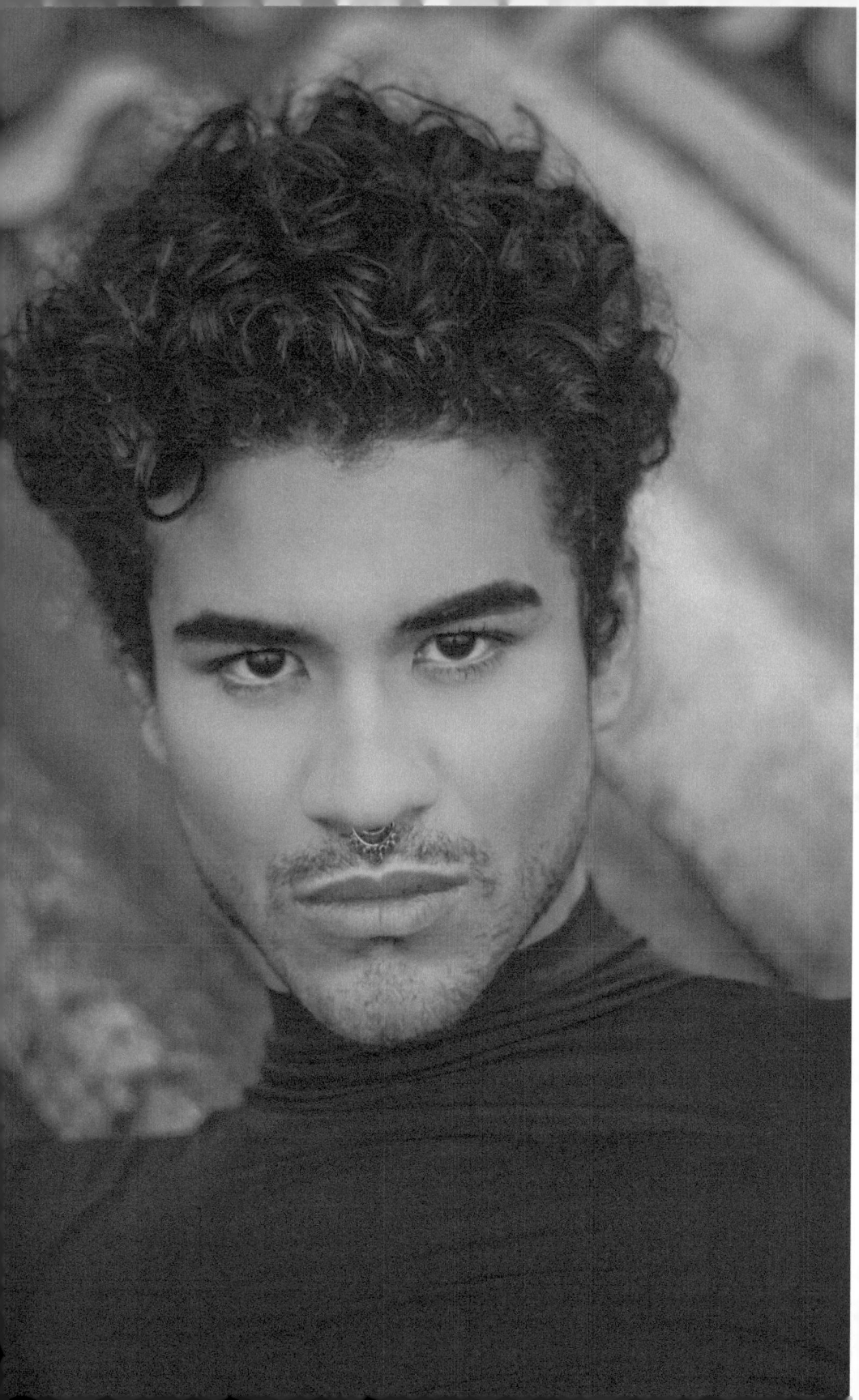

"Turn your face to the sun and the shadows fall behind you."

Unknown

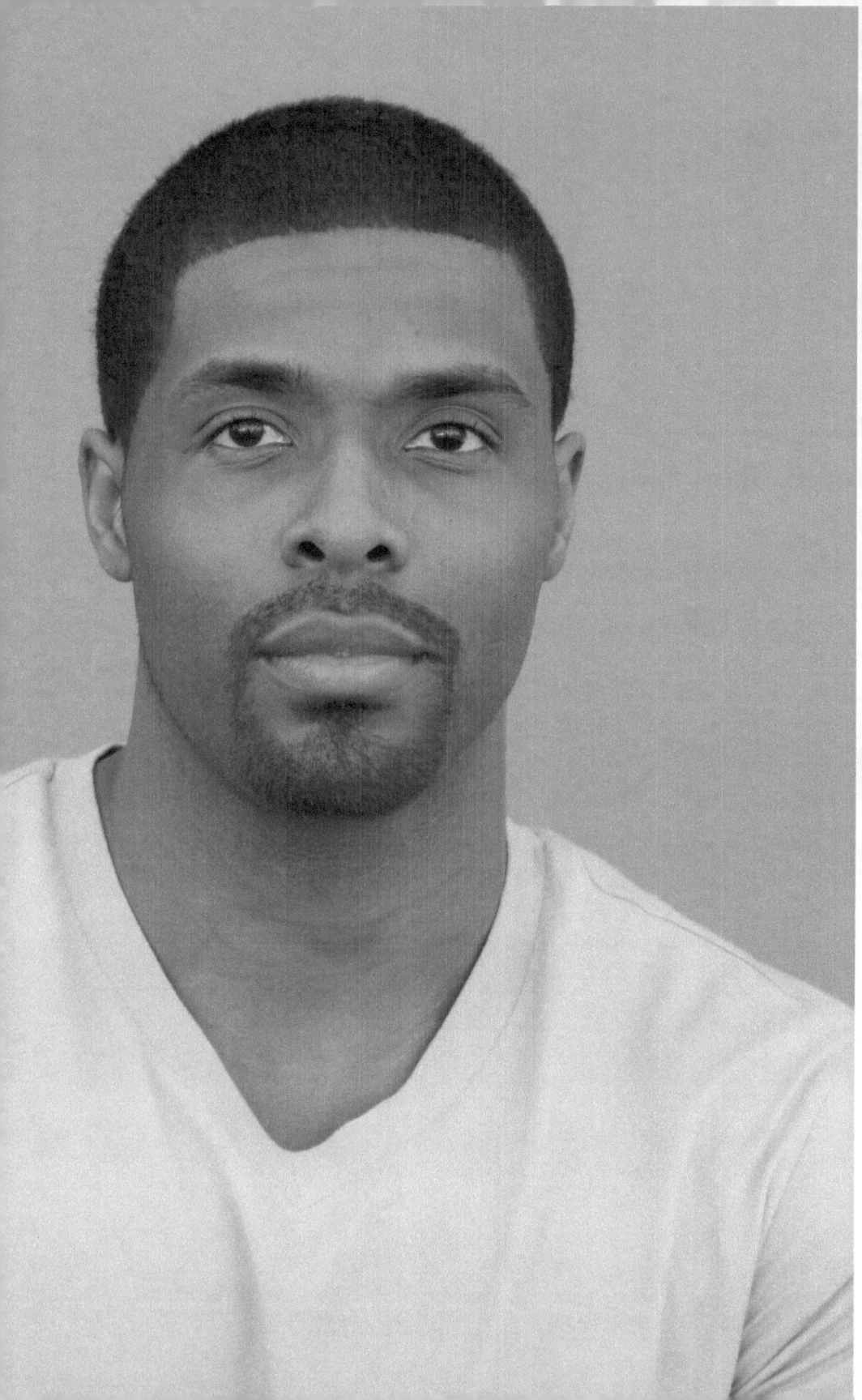

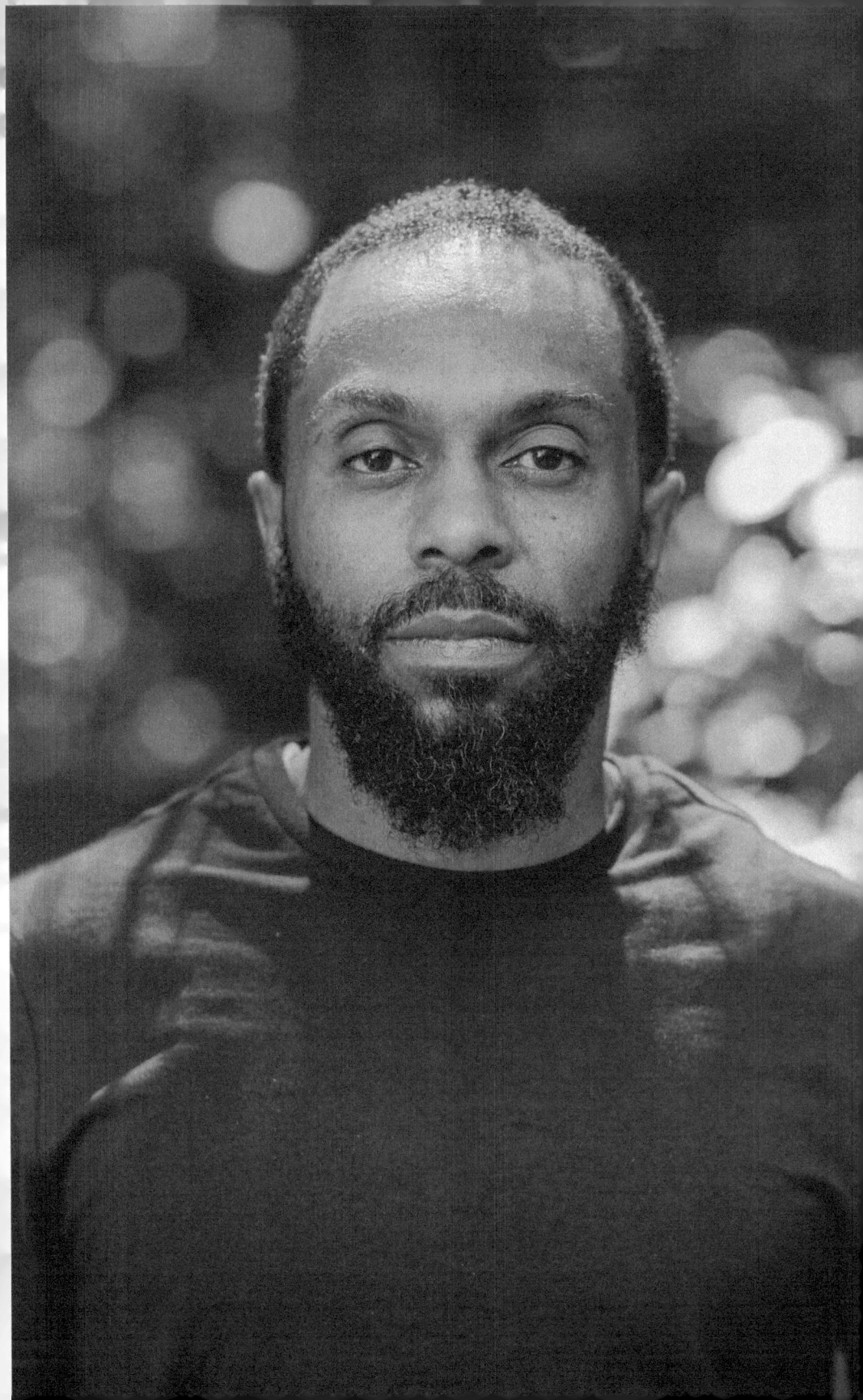

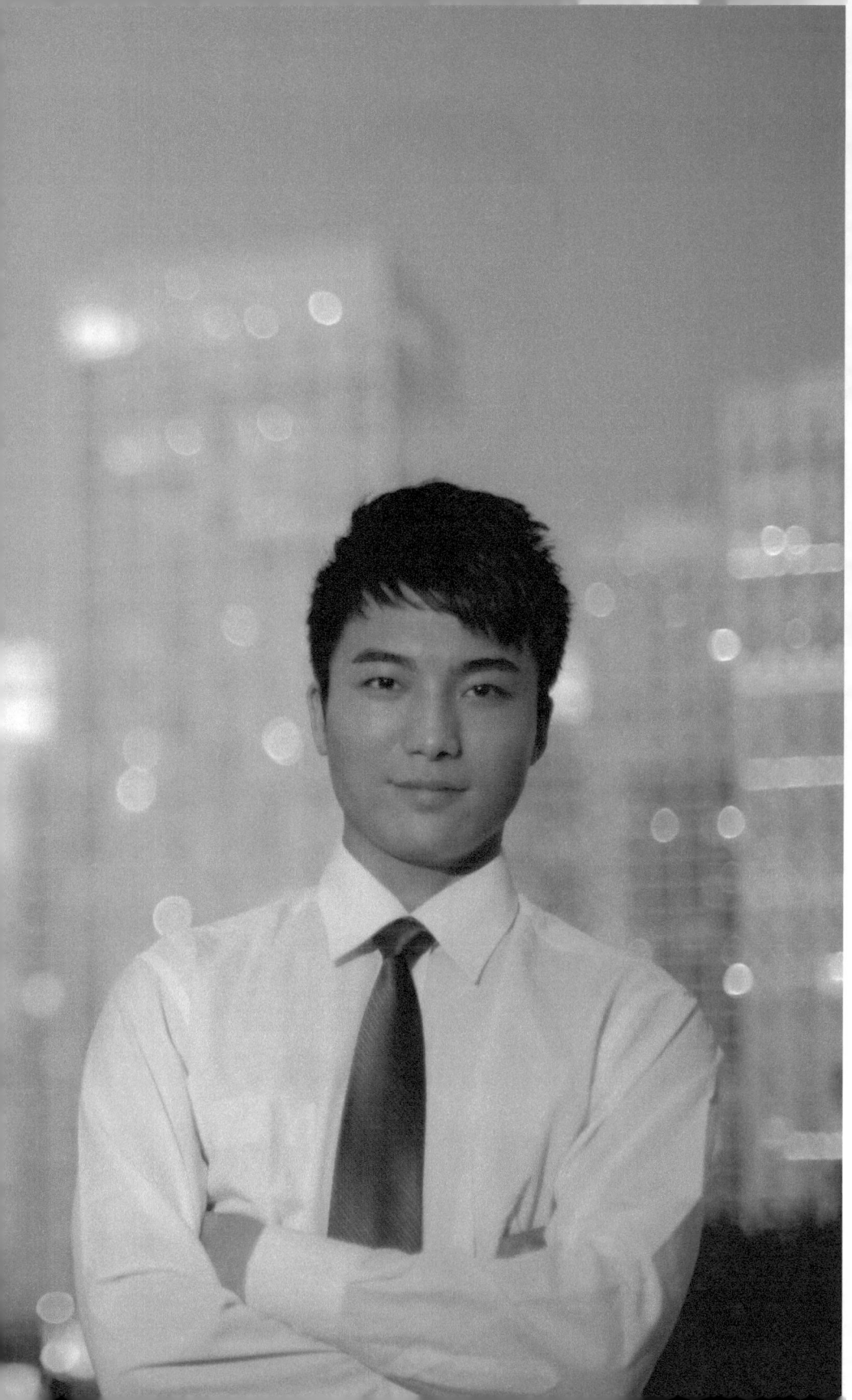

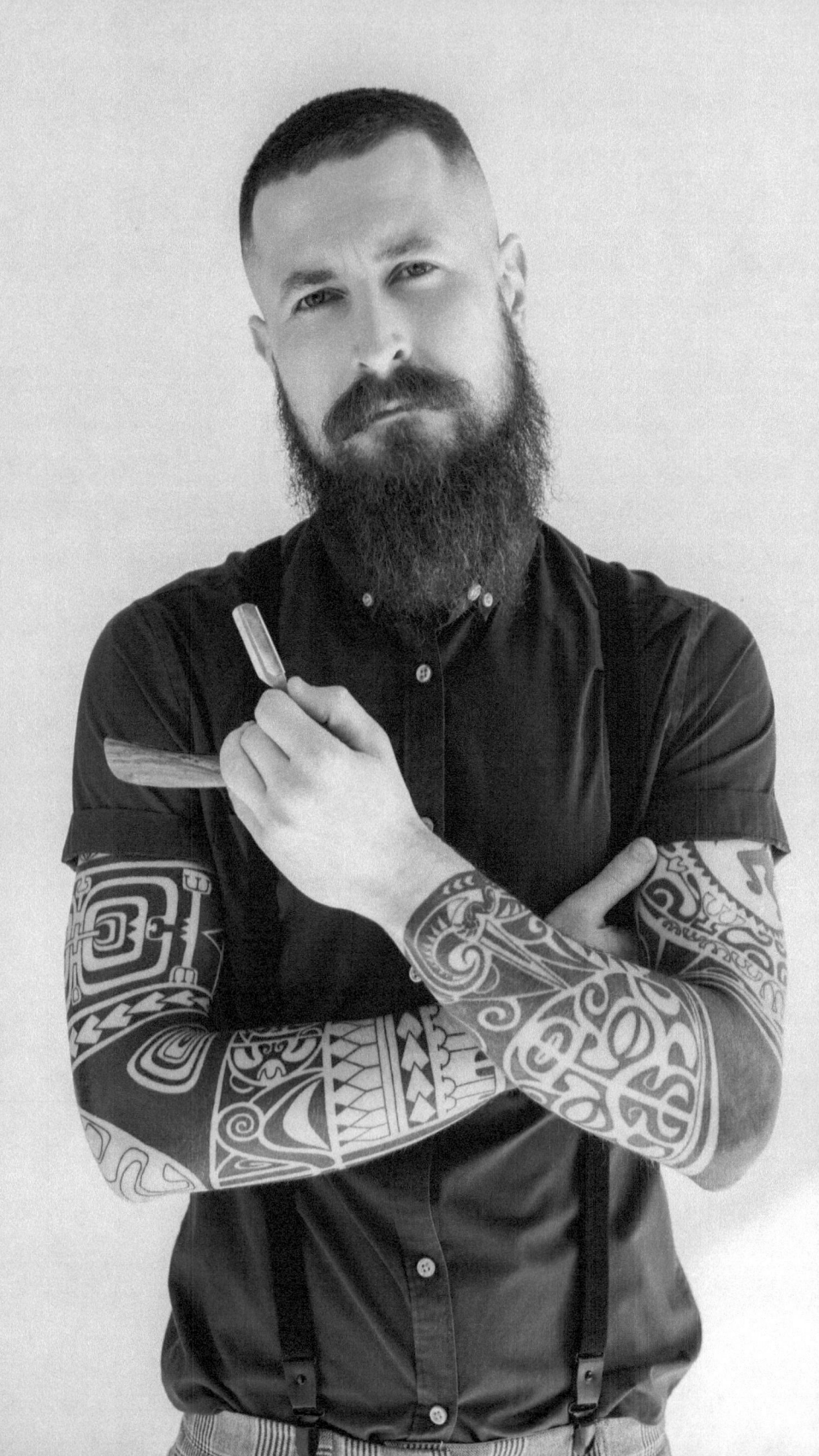

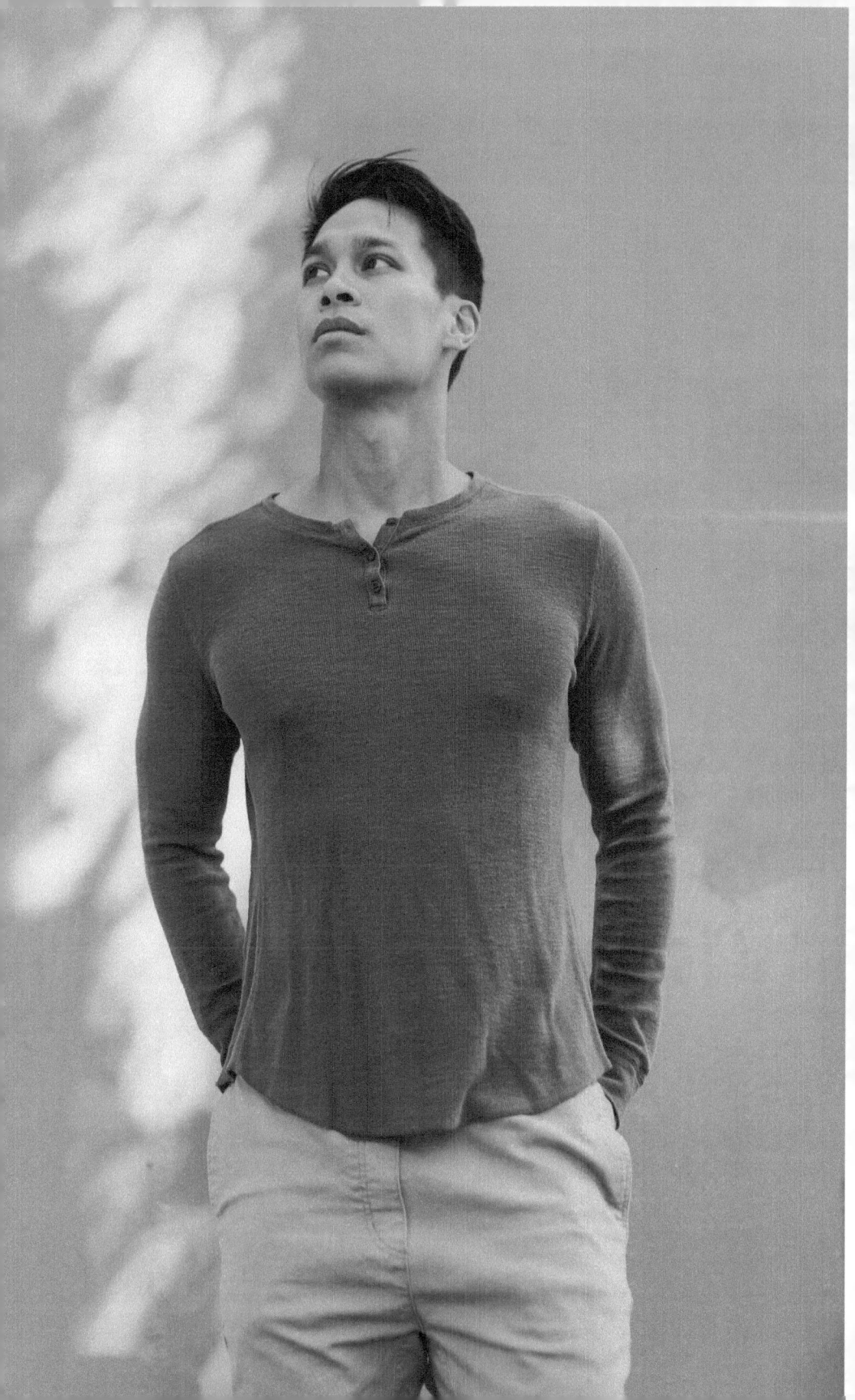

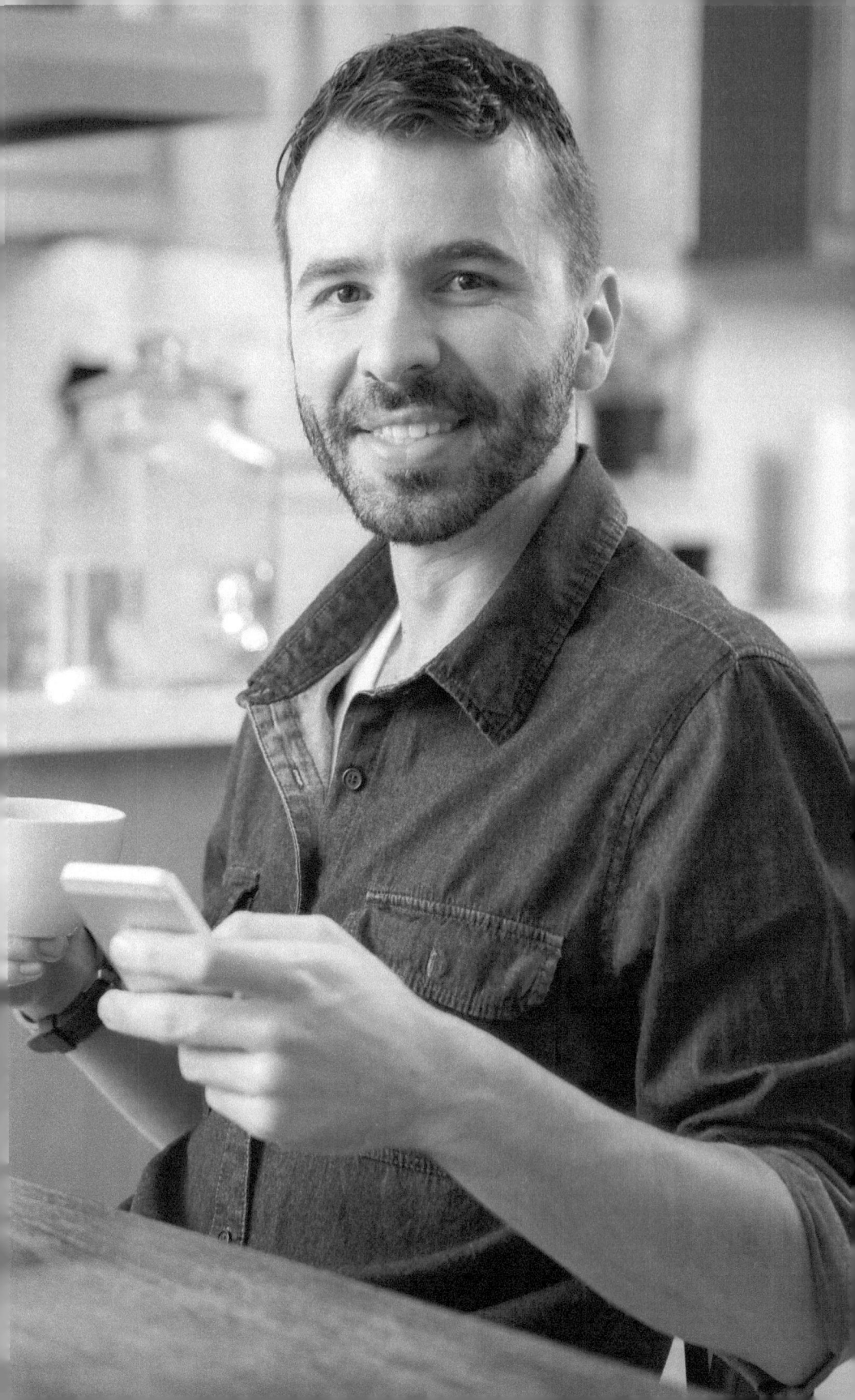

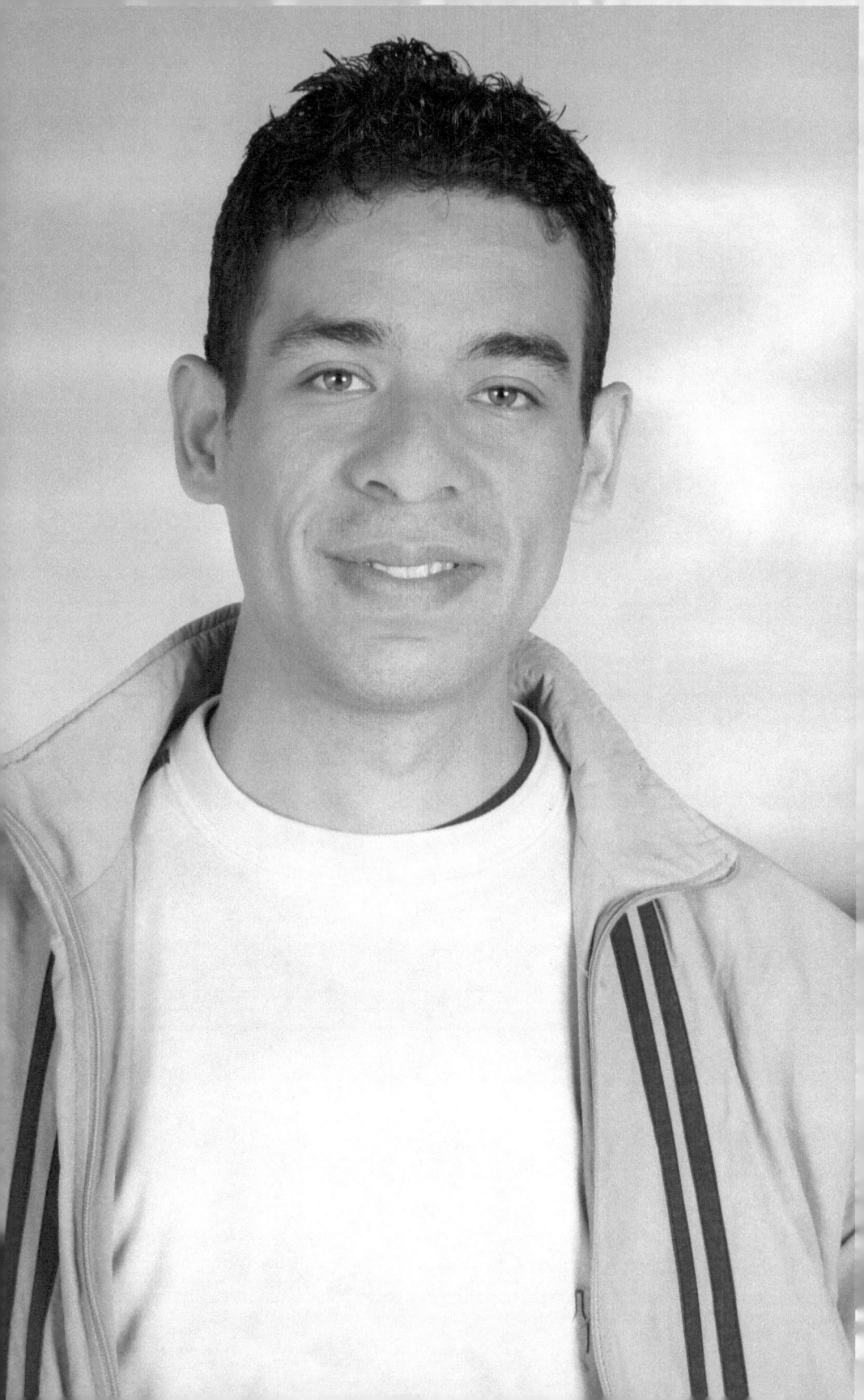

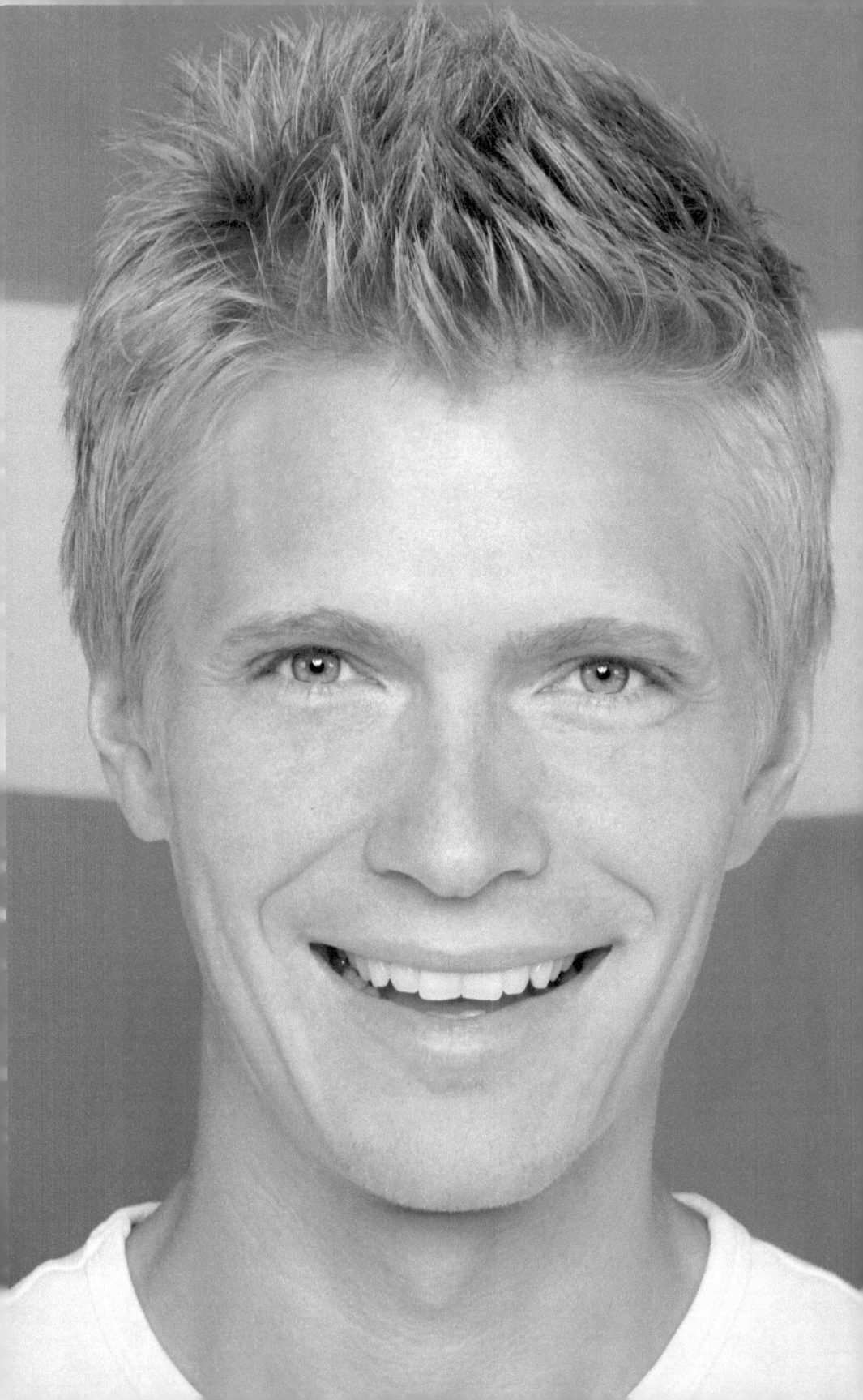

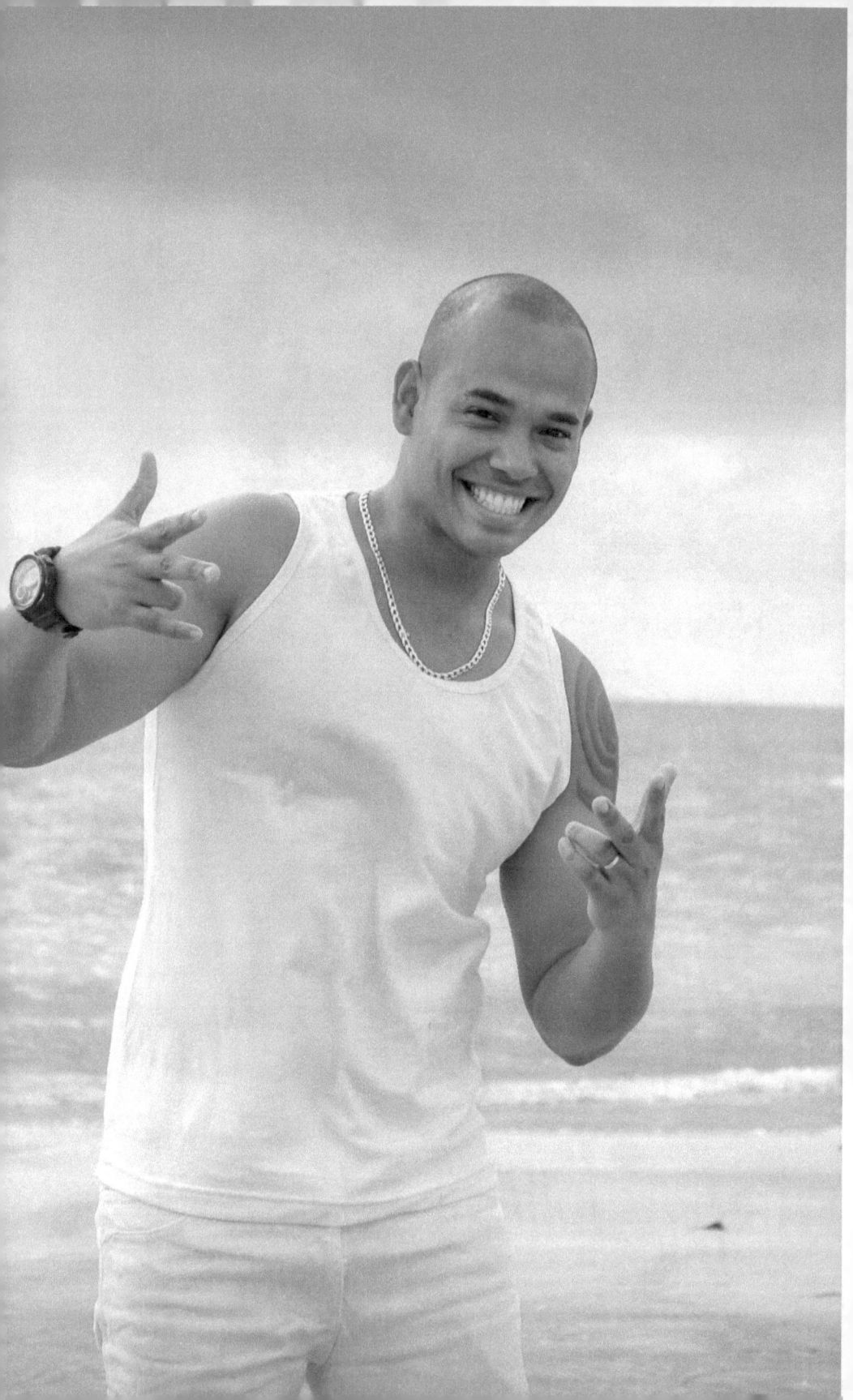

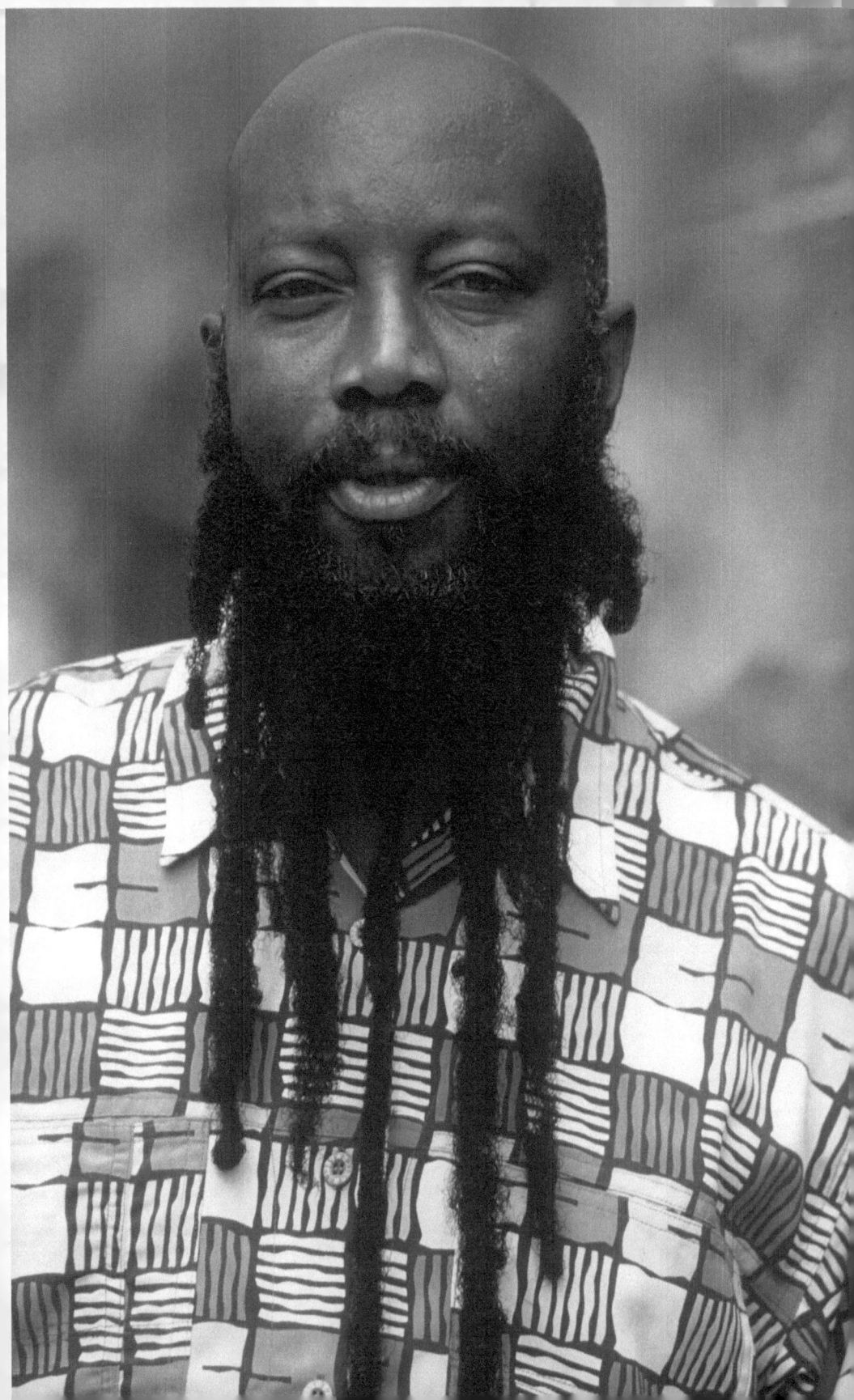

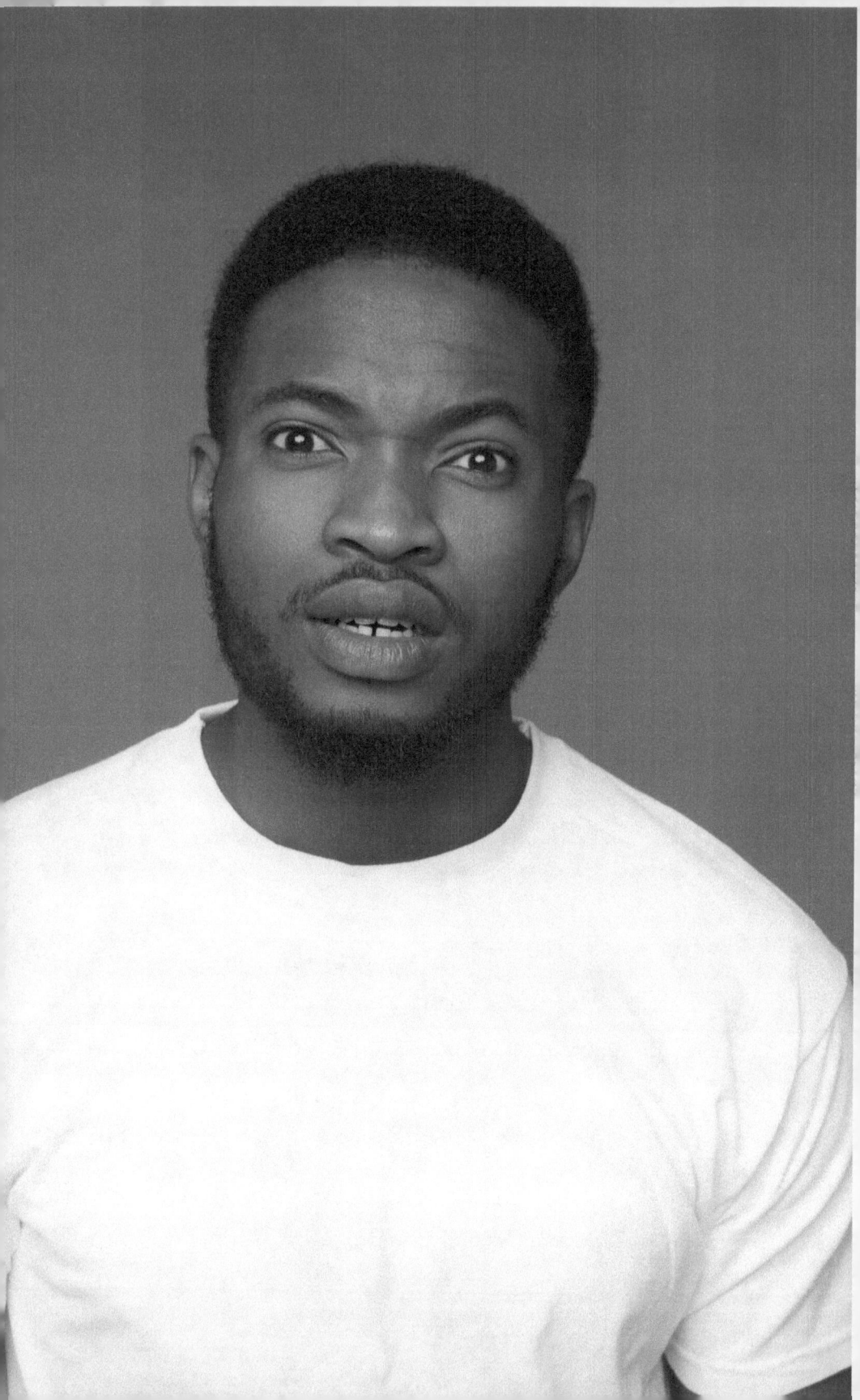

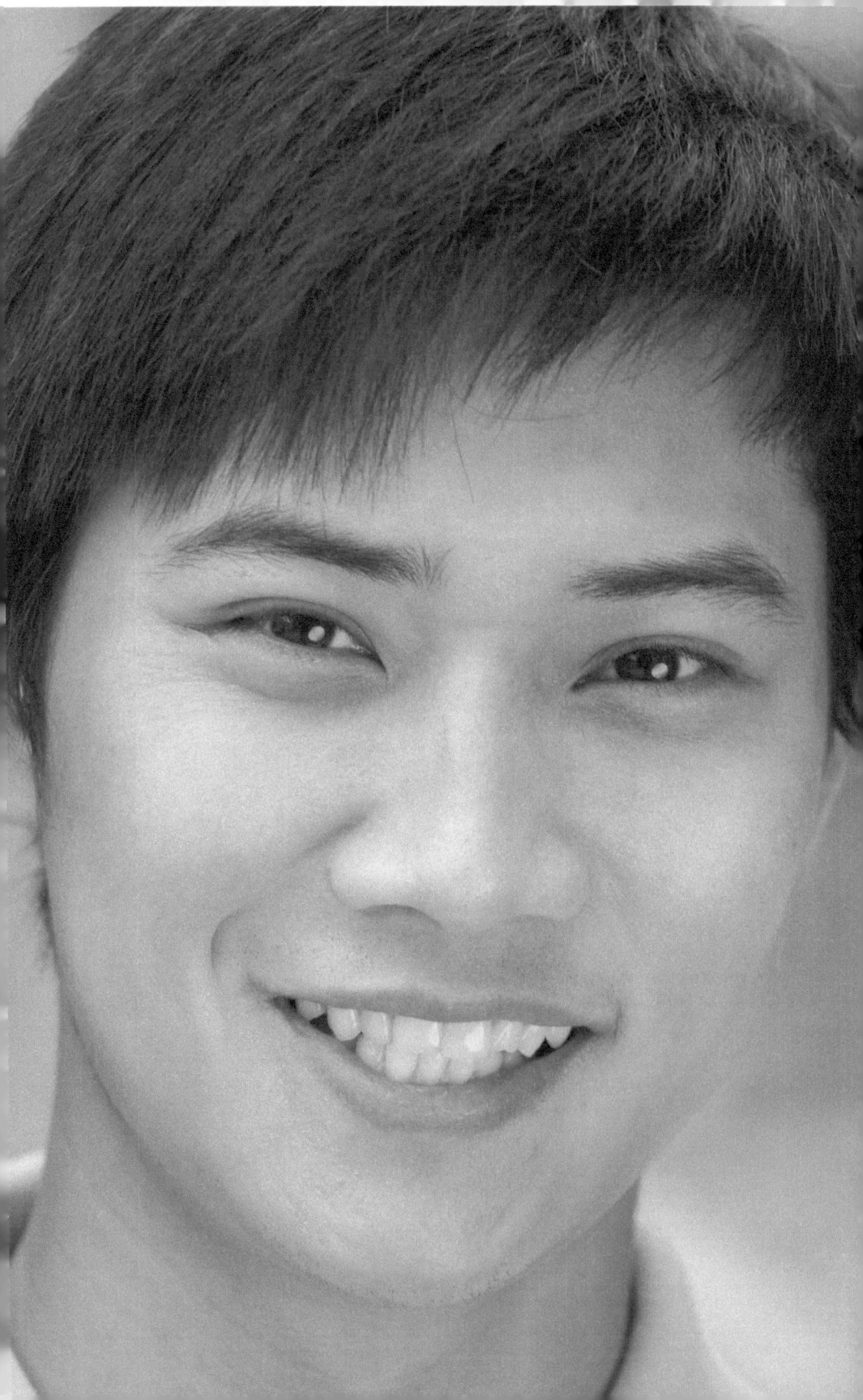

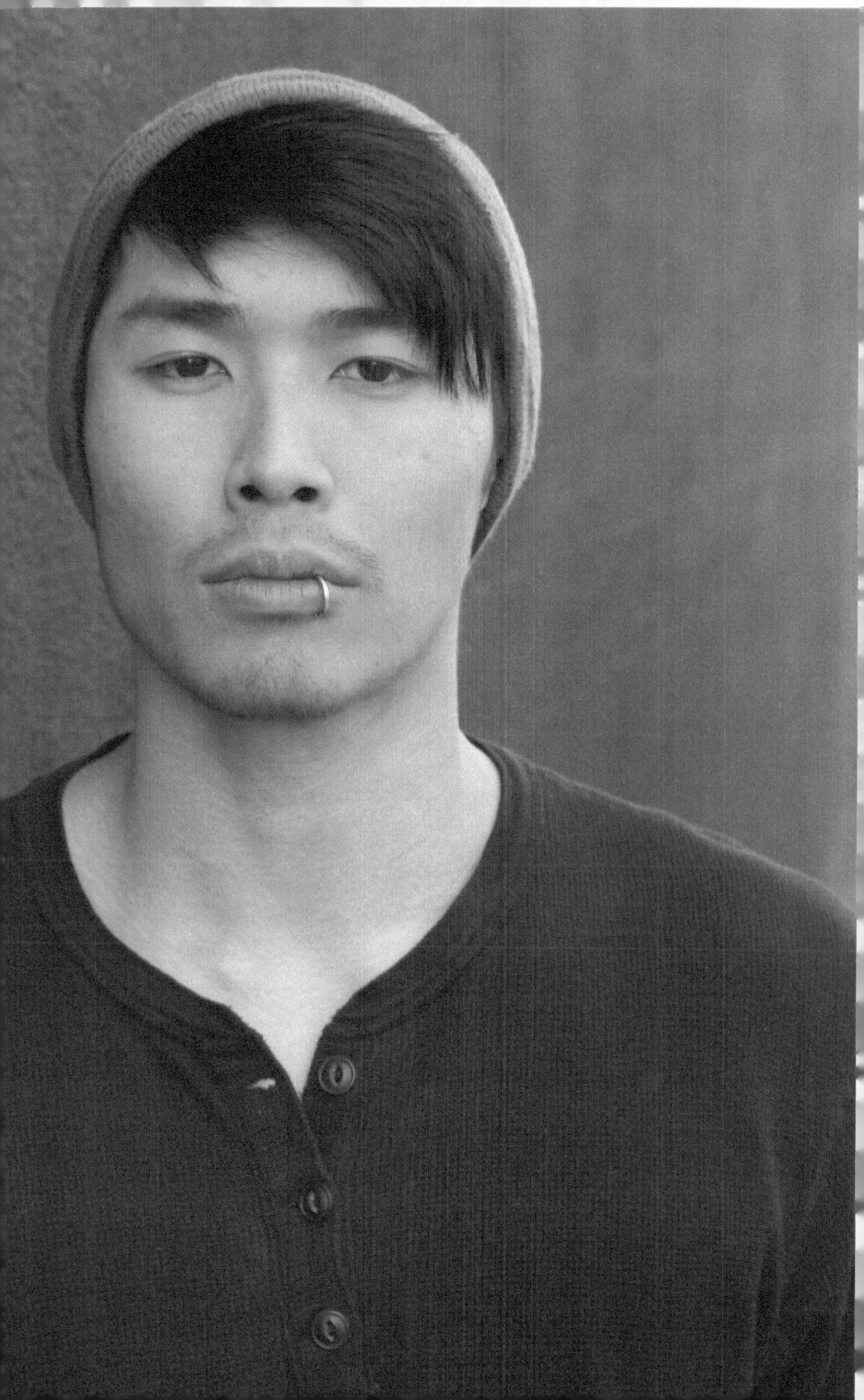

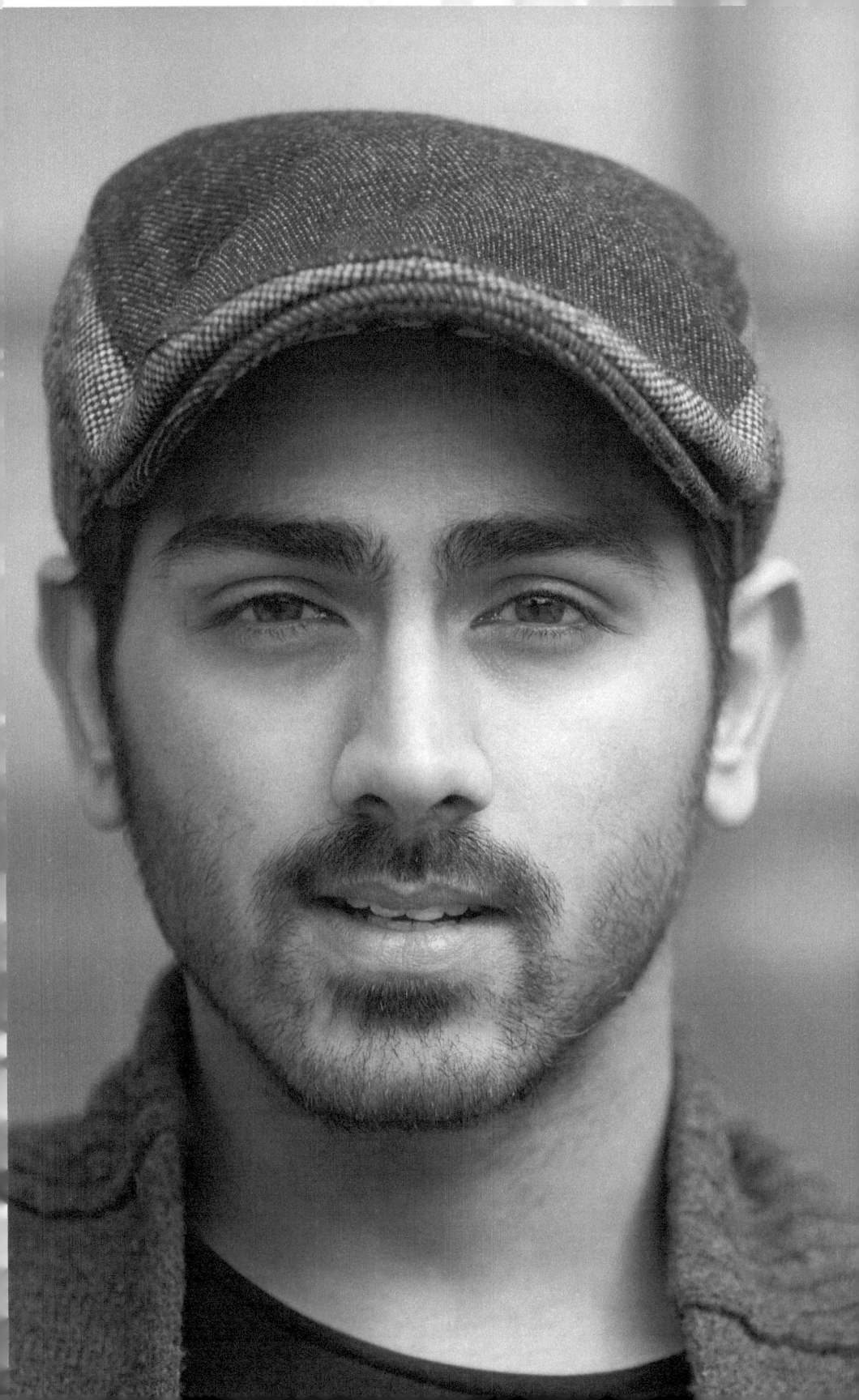

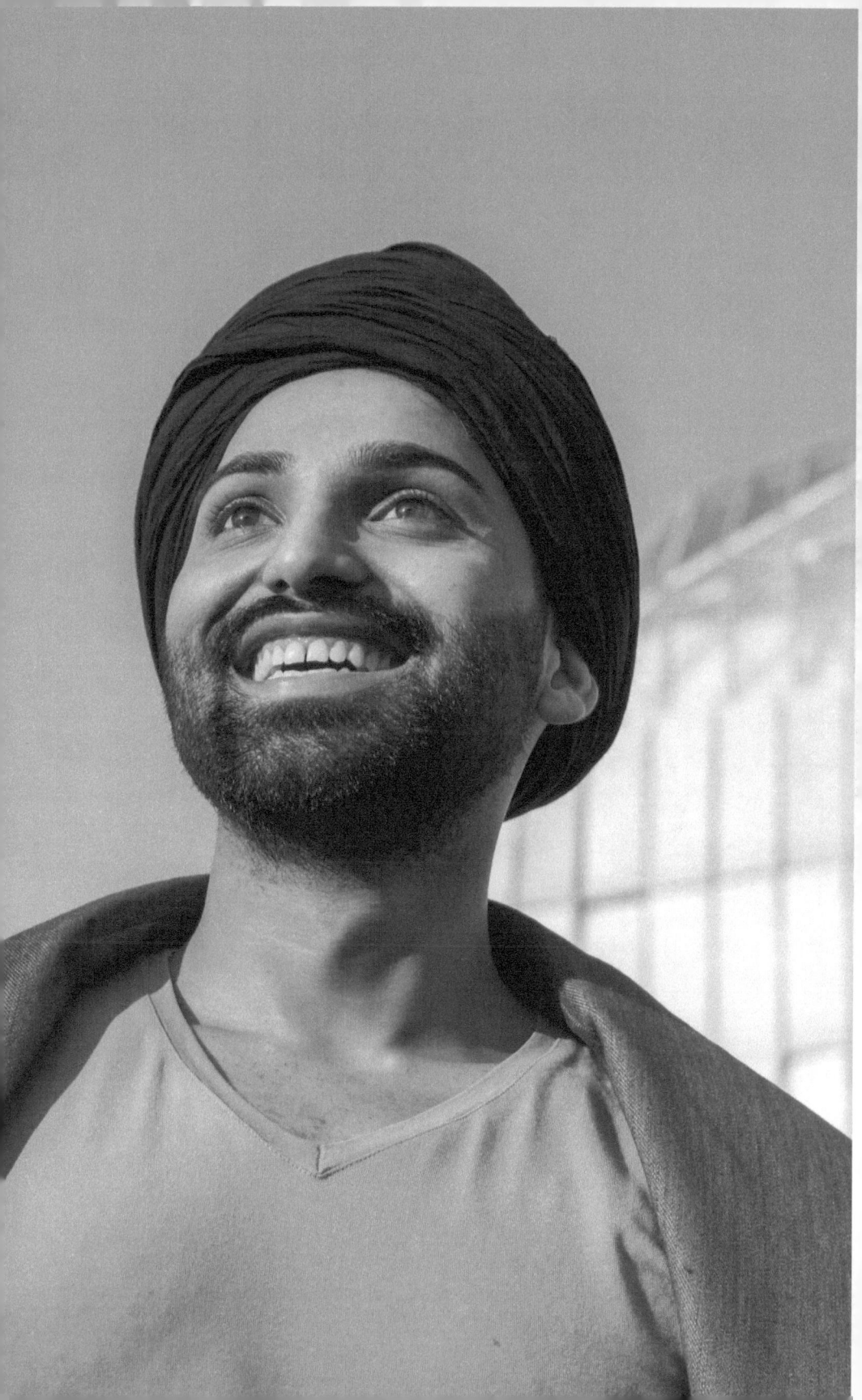

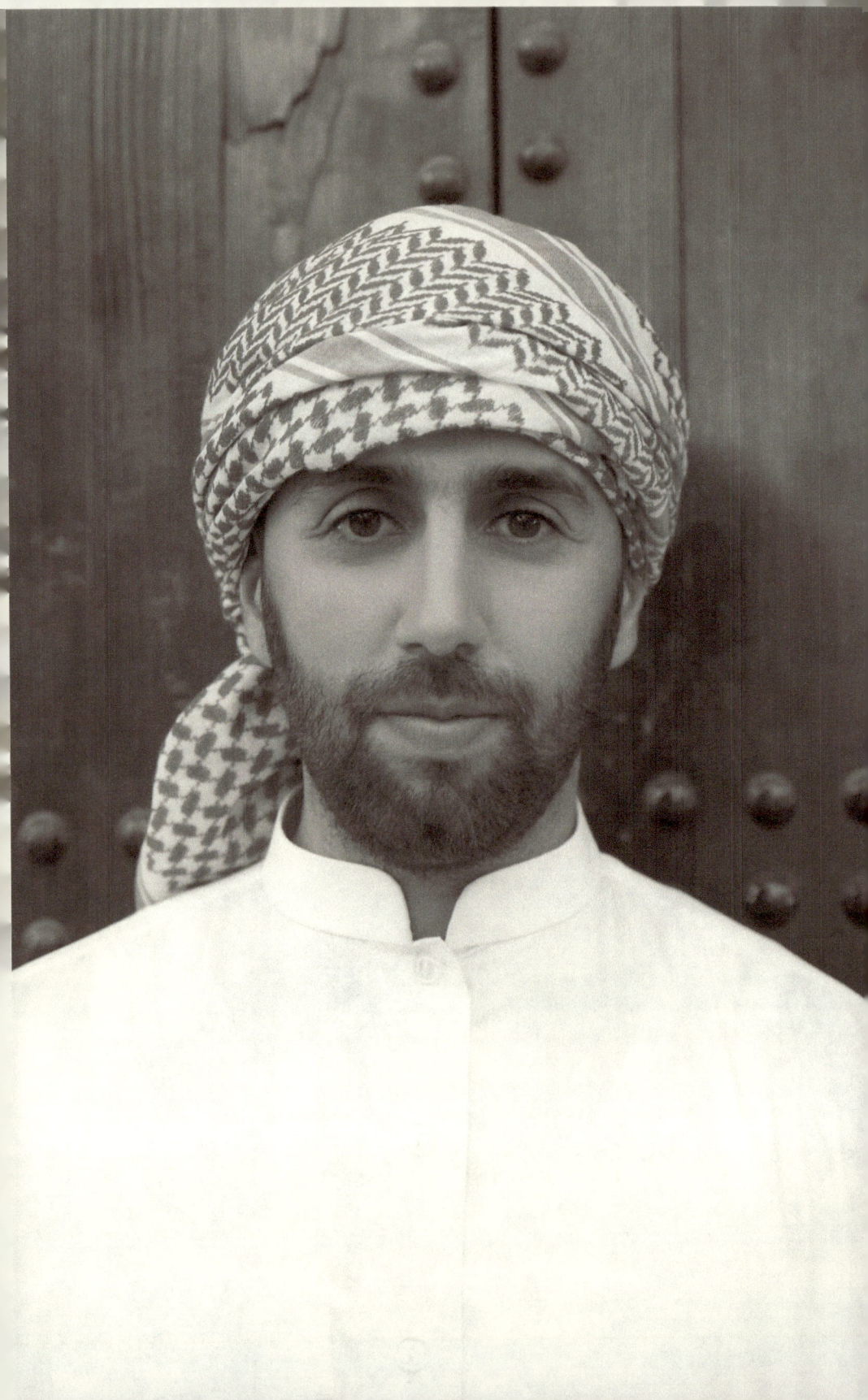

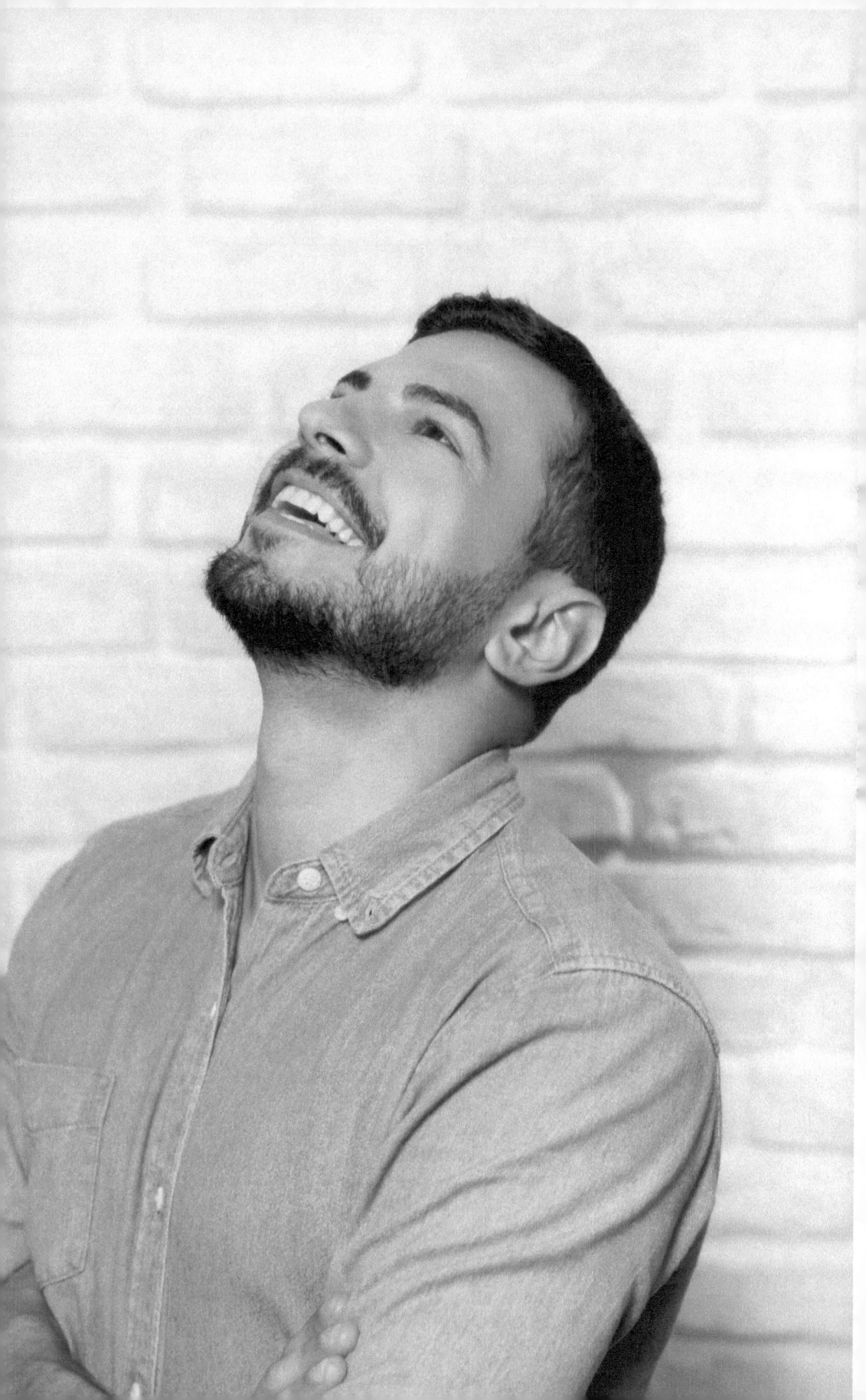

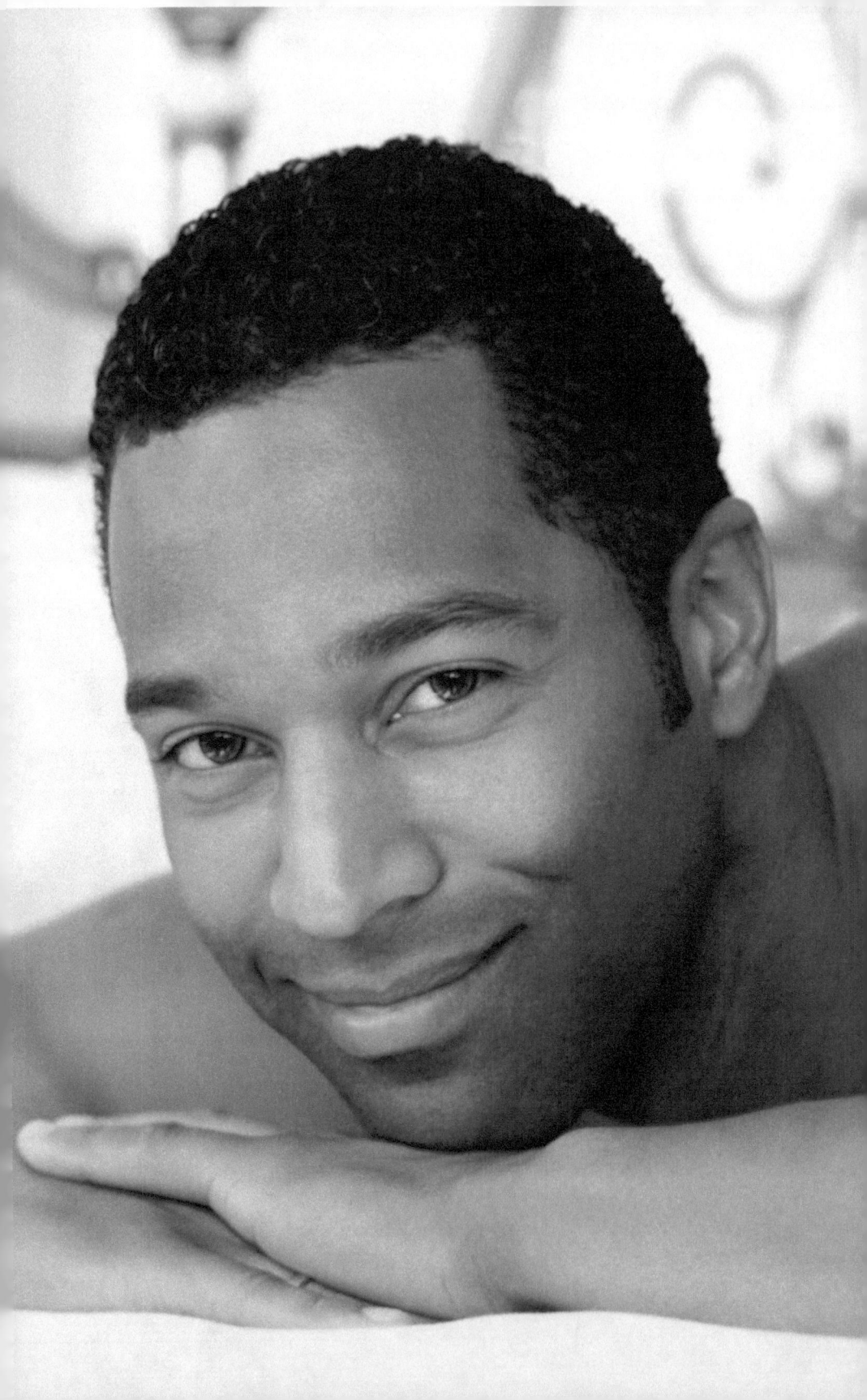

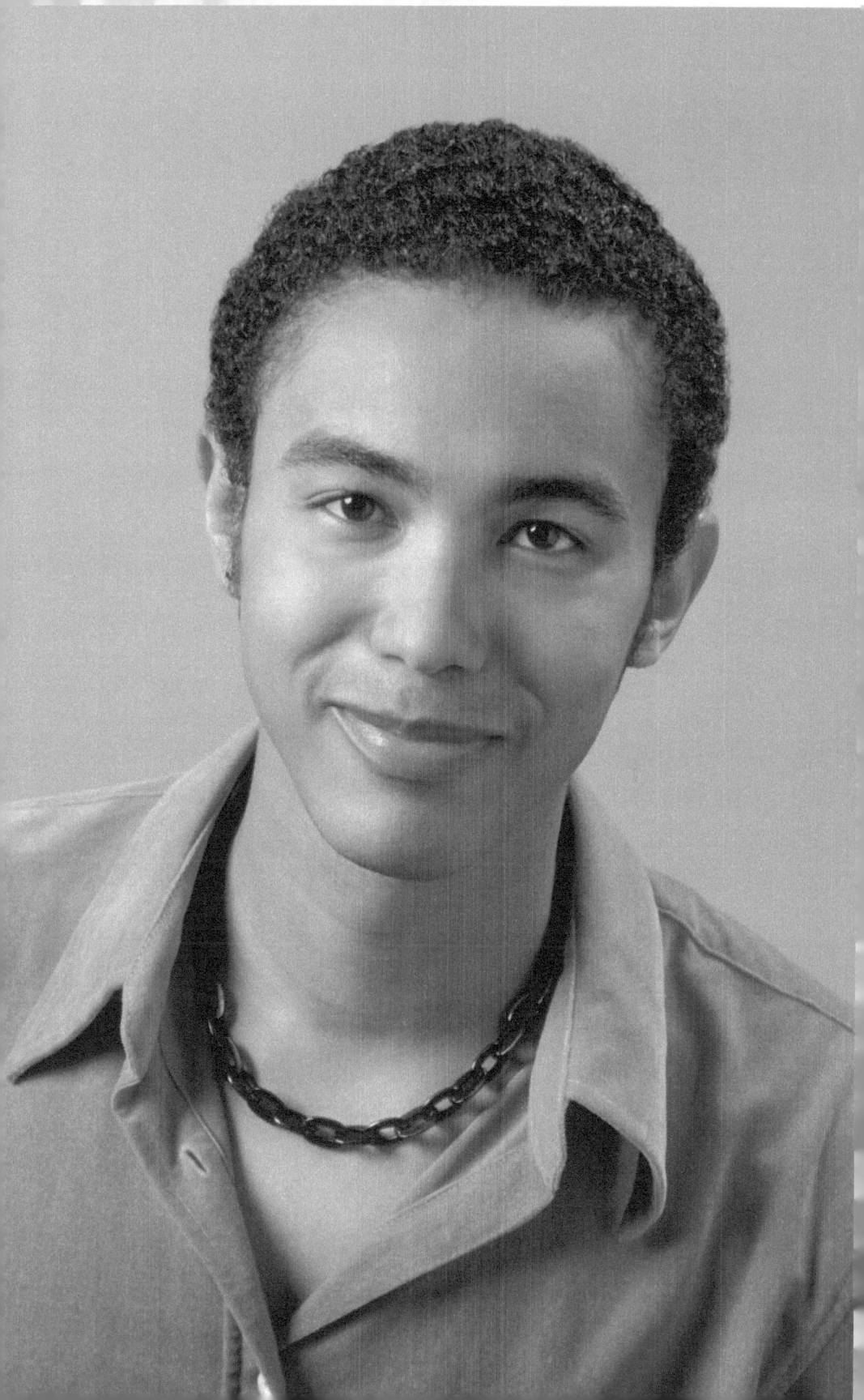

"ALL FACES ARE PERFECT"

BY ME

www.ingramcontent.com/pod-product-compliance
Lightning Source LLC
Chambersburg PA
CBHW030914180526
45163CB00004B/1832